Praise for *Small Acts of Grace*

"In a very warm and personal style, Alice Gray lets you look over her shoulder as she reveals some of her own acts of grace as well as those from other contributors. In her very readable style, you will enjoy and be encouraged by every chapter."

EMILIE BARNES, Speaker, Author, and
Founder of "More Hours in My Day"

"If you are looking for some sprinkles of sunshine to brighten your day, encourage your soul, and inspire you to touch others with the love of Jesus, then this is the book for you. Alice Gray has once again written a treasure of a book that you'll want to read over and over again. It will change your life."

LYSA TERKEURST, Author, Speaker, and
President of Proverbs 31 Ministries

"After spending an evening reading *Small Acts of Grace* I've never felt so motivated to, as Alice so charmingly writes, 'scatter sunshine' into the lives of others. I can hardly wait until morning to perform a few small acts of grace of my own. When you read this book you'll know exactly what I mean!"

SUSAN WALES, Best-selling Author
Social Graces and *A Match Made in Heaven*

"I am amazed at Alice Gray's insight into the hearts of women. I can truly relate to her words of encouragement and challenging stories."

CYNTHIA BEEDE, Youth Pastor's Wife

"Alice Gray's words of encouragement are like seeds planted in the heart so we can make a difference in the lives of others."

KAREN JAMISON, Cancer Support Group Leader

"Even if you think you are ministry impaired, this book will give you vision and a gentle push to follow the dreams God has given you."

ERIN JOHANNESEN, Nurse and Mother of Three

"'It's hard to sprinkle sunshine on others without getting some on yourself.' With encouragement like this, Alice Gray shares how remarkably easy it is to lay a foundation of grace in the hearts of those around us. As believers in Christ we are called to be salt and light in this world, and *Small Acts of Grace* clearly demonstrates how."

KIM MEEDER, Author of *Hope Rising* and
Co-founder of Crystal Peaks Youth Ranch

"What a wonderful find! *Small Acts of Grace* gives practical ways for *every* woman to make a positive difference in the world around her! Many times when we think about making a difference, we think of big things that take a lot of time or money, but Alice Gray shows us that it's the little genuine things that we do for others that sometimes have the biggest effect! This book is a must have for women!"

MELANIE SCOTT, College Student

"This book contains so much warmth and practical wisdom. You'll cherish your copy and want to share it with the women who mean the most to you."

DOREEN BUTTON, Mother and Student

"*Small Acts of Grace* is a delightful 'must read' for women who desire to be used by God to make a difference in the lives of others."

KAREN ELLISON, Pastor's Wife and Women's Ministry Mentor

"Oh . . . if each of us would strive to make even a tiny difference in our everyday world, think how wonderful the whole world could be. Alice Gray shows us how. Read *Small Acts of Grace,* and start making a difference in your world."

NANCY HARRIS, Bible Study Teacher

"The ideas in this book are practical and 'doable.' It makes you want to go out in the world and make a difference one small act of grace at a time."

ELIZABETH HIGHTOWER, Director of Women's Ministries

SMALL ACTS OF
Grace

Blessings!
Alice Grace
9/6/08

OTHER BOOKS BY ALICE GRAY

SMALL ACTS OF

YOU CAN
MAKE A DIFFERENCE
IN EVERYDAY,
ORDINARY WAYS

ALICE GRAY

W PUBLISHING GROUP
A Division of Thomas Nelson Publishers
Since 1798

www.wpublishinggroup.com

Published by W Publishing Group, a Division of Thomas Nelson, Inc., P.O. Box 141000, Nashville, Tennessee 37214.

Library of Congress Cataloging-in-Publication Data

Gray, Alice, 1939–
    Small acts of grace : making a difference in everyday, ordinary ways / Alice Gray.
      p. cm.
    Includes bibliographical references.
    ISBN 0-8499-0448-X
    1. Christian women—Prayer-books and devotions—English. 2. Christian women—
Religious life. I. Title.
BV4844.G745 2006
242'.643—dc22
                          2006005680

For all the women who have
made a difference in my life.
And to my sister, Nola,
who introduced me to Jesus.

Contents

A Special Thank-You

*T*o eight women from across the country who took time to read and evaluate an early manuscript—Cindy Beede, Doreen Button, Karen L. Ellison, Nancy Harris, Elizabeth D. Hightower, Karen Jamison, Erin Johannesen, and Melanie Scott . . . *I deeply appreciate your valuable suggestions.*

To my editor, Anne Christian Buchanan . . . *You are incredible! It is a tremendous blessing to work with the best of the best.*

To Debbie Wickwire at W Publishing . . . *Thank you for your trustworthy guidance and for cheering me on.*

To my husband, Al Gray . . . *How could I manage without you? Every single day you find ways to love, care for, encourage, and protect me. And, even after all these years, when you hear our love song, you still ask me to dance.*♡

To my Lord and Savior Jesus Christ . . . *Although this book is but a small act of grace, my prayer is that it will bring You pleasure.*

A NOTE TO MY READERS

$\mathscr{I}$ have used many true stories in this book. Sometimes I changed the names and altered the circumstances to protect the privacy of the people involved.

PROLOGUE

Follow His Heart

He is the Truth to be told.
The Way to be walked.
The Light to be lit.

MOTHER TERESA

Although it was only April, the early morning sun felt warm on my face. Soft breezes stirred the cherry trees, and an occasional blossom floated down and landed in my hair like pink confetti. I was sitting on a park bench not far from our home in Oregon. It was a perfect spot for thinking—and I couldn't get one particular question out of my mind.

The day before, our pastor had closed the worship service by asking, "When you get to heaven, what will Jesus say about you?" It was as if someone had suddenly switched all the questions.

From the time I was a little girl in pigtails up through my adult years, the questions had always been about what *I* wanted to be, what *my* goals and ambitions were, and how *I* wanted people to remember me when I was gone. But on that Sunday morning nearly twelve years ago, my pastor's question began to change the focus of all my answers.

It was no longer about what I wanted, but about what Jesus wanted to do through my life. About whether I would fulfill my own dreams, or whether I would fulfill the dreams He had for me.

As I thought about our pastor's question, my mind raced ahead, wondering what it would be like when I stepped on heaven's shore and saw my Savior for the first time. Could it ever be possible that He would open His arms and say,

"Welcome home, dear one; you are a woman who followed My heart."

Oh, that is my longing—my deepest desire. To walk in *His* footsteps and to follow *His* heart. To respond to His magnificent acts of grace in my life with my own small acts of grace that make a difference in the world around me.

I imagine the same is true for you.

I wish we were sitting side by side on that same park bench with cherry blossoms falling in our hair. We could talk about this together. I would love to hear about the ways you listen to God's voice and how you are following the dreams He has given you. What have been the highest peaks and deepest valleys of your life? What did you learn about following the Lord's heart during those times? And what have you learned about following Him in the ordinary moments of your everyday life?

As I write, I have tried to imagine some of the things you might say—the encouragement and help you would offer to me. And, in turn, I've prayed and asked the Lord what He might want me to share with you. So come along, walk with me through the pages of this book . . . and together we'll discover how small acts of grace can make a difference in our world.

CHAPTER 1

Parade of Lights

This little light of mine,
I'm going to let it shine,
Let it shine, let it shine, let it shine.

FROM AN OLD SPIRITUAL

*W*hile vacationing in Southern California, we spent a day at Disneyland and stayed until the park closed at midnight. One of our favorite attractions was the Electric Light Parade on Main Street. Every day at half-past darkness, the lights along the parade route dimmed, and toe-tapping music blared through strategically placed loudspeakers. The adults stood on tiptoe, daddies lifted young children to their shoulders, and everyone squeezed a little closer to the front row of spectators.

When the first glittering float came into view, the youngest toddlers to the oldest grandparents clapped their hands in sheer delight. For twenty minutes, an array of twirling Disney characters, brass marching bands, and a dozen magical floats draped with thousands of shimmering lights paraded down Main Street.

It was an incredibly happy experience. No wonder they call it the Magic Kingdom!

The following week, I described the parade to one of my Christian friends. "Alice," she said, leaning close to me, "I think God wants us to be like that light parade."

What a profound and wonderful thought—to think that we might bring that kind of joy to the main streets of our towns.

LET IT SHINE

Right after the Beatitudes, just fourteen verses into what is commonly called the Sermon on the Mount, Jesus tells His followers—including us—that each of us is the light of the world.

> You are the light of the world—like a city on a mountain, glowing in the night for all to see. Don't hide your light under a basket! Instead, put it on a stand and let it shine for all. In the same way, let your good deeds shine out for all to see, so that everyone will praise your heavenly Father.[1]

I think it is incredibly awesome to be called the light of the world. And not just because that's a whole lot better than being called the *dark* of the world—but because light is the very picture Jesus used to describe Himself! Look at this verse from the Gospel of John: "Then Jesus spoke to them again, saying, 'I am the light of the world.'"[2]

> *There are two ways of spreading light; to be the candle or the mirror that reflects it.*
>
> EDITH WHARTON

When I consider that Jesus described us the same way He portrayed Himself—well, that changes everything about everything. I can't even begin to put in words what it means to me. I just know that I feel both honored and unworthy to bear such a name. And I long to bring pleasure to the One who calls me "light."

4

But what exactly does it *mean* to be the light of the world? To answer that, I think we need to take a look at what light does. It can be a beacon of safety, a lamp of comfort, a candle of hope. But its primary purpose is dispelling darkness.

One weekend years ago, our family visited the Oregon Caves National Monument, which is famous for its network of marble caverns. A tour guide took a group of about twenty of us deep into these caves—not a good place to visit when you are a bit claustrophobic, as I am.

The guide kept assuring us that there was an exit not too far down the path if any of us felt we needed to leave. Once he started talking about the bats roosting above us, I was counting the steps to that emergency exit. And yes, wimpy as I am, I gratefully took the exit a short while later. But before we got there, we continued deeper and deeper down the path and around so many curves that not one bit of outside light filtered in. There were only small pathway lights. My hands were clammy. Nausea gripped my stomach.

It was at this point that the guide made an unexpected announcement. He was going to turn off the pathway lights for a moment so we could experience total darkness. We were not to worry because he had a powerful flashlight in case something happened and the lights didn't come back on. I fumbled for my husband's hand and found it just as the lights went out.

I'm sure the darkness lasted only seconds, but it felt like forever. And then, just when I thought I couldn't stand it one moment longer, someone else struggling with the darkness struck a match. One single glorious match. Oh, such a relief! Only that one small light—but what a difference it made.

I often think of that moment when I hear the morning news and read the headlines in the paper. The world does seem to be growing darker these days. But my experience in the Oregon Caves reminds me that the darker the place, the brighter my little light can shine.

FIRST THINGS FIRST

In God's Word, light is associated with joy and blessings. But perhaps more important, light in Scripture often refers to God's presence. "The LORD is my light and my salvation," proclaims Psalm 27:1, while Isaiah adds, "The people who walked in darkness have seen a great light." And Paul wrote to the Christians in Corinth that God "shone in our hearts to give the light of the knowledge of the glory of God."[3]

How essential, therefore, to spend some quiet time with Him each day—talking to Him, listening to His voice, reading His Word, inviting Him to be part of our day, and simply relaxing in the awareness that He is here with us. That's how we learn to shine—by spending time in the light of His presence.

Unfortunately, in our hectic, hurry-up, keep-doing-more world, all this is easier to desire than to do.

An exhausted mother wakes up early, determined to spend time with the Lord before her children get up. Still groggy, she kneels down in front of a living-room chair, rests her forehead on her arms, and unwillingly falls asleep before her first prayer request is finished.

A career woman starts multitasking the second her alarm

jars her awake. Listening to voice mail while she dresses, eating on the run, putting on makeup in the car, she hopes to find a quiet time when she gets back home. But by six that evening her energy is spent and her tote bag is bulging with unfinished projects brought home from the office.

The retired woman *knows* the popular image of lounging in her bathrobe and reading her Bible while sipping her second cup of coffee isn't true for her. Her schedule is somehow busier than ever with family (love those grandchildren!), volunteering at church and in the community, and other activities she always wanted to do but never had time to. And yet she lacks the energy of her younger counterparts. Even now, efforts to carve out a regular quiet time seem to fall by the wayside.

So what's a woman to do? As difficult as it seems, we must somehow find a way to quiet

> *Too often, the brightest light in many women's lives is the candle they are burning on both ends.*
>
> MARY WELCHEL

our hearts before the Lord. God's Word tells us this is our first priority: "Seek *first* the kingdom of God and His righteousness, and all these things shall be added to you."[4] And in my own life, I find that the battles of my day are often won or lost depending on whether or not I find some quiet moments to sit at the feet of Jesus.

If you struggle in this area, maybe one of the following suggestions will help:

For the exhausted mom: Try keeping your Bible open on

the kitchen counter and choose one or two verses a day to inspire you. Sing them out loud while you pack lunches and do the dishes. Pray for your family as you make beds and fold clothes. Then keep trying to find a few times during the week when you can spend a longer time in God's Word.

For the career woman: Since you are probably good at keeping appointments, try blocking off a daily appointment with the Lord. Find a time early in the day when you have more energy to quiet your heart and hear His voice. When you drive to work, listen to worship music instead of the news. If the neighborhood is safe and the weather pleasant, arrive at work a little early so you can put on headphones and walk for ten or fifteen minutes listening to the Bible on CD.[5]

For the retired woman: As much as you love giving and serving and enjoying new activities, perhaps you must learn to say no sometimes. If you are feeling worn out and can't find time to spend with the Lord, try saying something like, "Thank you so much for asking me. Although I would love to do it in the future, I really must say no this time." If you say it sweetly, I guarantee you'll be asked again!

I think we sometimes forget that not only does God want to be an active part of our everyday lives, but He is the *reason* we can shine at all. I love Psalm 18:28 because it makes the point so clear: "For You cause my lamp to be lighted and to shine; the Lord my God illumines my darkness."[6]

Try reading the verse again, and this time think about your favorite lamp. Picture the lamp when it's off, and then picture how different it is when you turn it on. That's what the Lord does for us. Isn't that a wonderful thought?

One time when I was teaching a women's Bible study, I used two vintage oil lamps to demonstrate how this verse works in our lives. One lamp had only a little oil in the base—too little oil for the wick to reach, so the wick was stiff and dry. The other lamp was nearly full, with the wick totally saturated in the oil. Both lamps were beautiful, with ribbed pedestals, elegant clear glass fonts, and fluted chimneys. But when it came to actually shining, they couldn't have been more different.

It was difficult to light the dry wick, and when it finally did catch, there was no flame, only a bit of glow that lasted for a few minutes at the most. The wick with the oil, on the other hand, caught the flame immediately and continued to burn brightly.

Your word is a lamp to my feet and a light to my path.

PSALM 119:105

I really don't need to make the application for you. You already get it. Too many missed days without an intimate time with the Lord, and we are like the lamp with the dry wick. We need to be saturated in the oil of His Word and soaked in His love so the Lord can cause our lives to shine.

GRACEFUL BEACONS

Because summer is so hot in Arizona, where we live now, my husband, Al, and I like to take our walks just after sunset. We usually carry a flashlight because streetlights weren't planned for our little town. Folks don't want them. They think most streetlights are harsh and rude, and they're more interested in seeing stars sparkling against a midnight sky. But one neighborhood did install gas lamps along their streets. Standing like graceful beacons, they glow gently in the darkness and give off just the right amount of light to make you feel warm and comfortable. It's pleasant to walk in that neighborhood at night.

I'd like it if people thought of me as a graceful beacon, wouldn't you?

I know there are times when I must stand up bravely and speak out for what I believe in. I don't want to hide my light. I want it to burn brightly for all to see. But, at the same time, I don't want to be like a bare bulb just hanging from the ceiling on an ugly cord or a harsh, buzzing streetlight. I pray that my glow will be so warm and attractive that it draws people into the comforting circle of Christ's love. I think that's exactly what Jesus had in mind when He told us to let our good deeds shine so that everyone will praise our heavenly Father.

> *The stars are the streetlights of eternity.*
>
> AUTHOR UNKNOWN

While writing this book, it has been my desire that every page will encourage women to be a lovely light for the Lord. I think the qualities the apostle Paul described as "the fruit of the Spirit"—love, joy, peace, longsuffering, kindness, goodness, faithfulness, gentleness, self-control[7]—also describe the kind of light God wants us to give forth. Because it is so unselfish, so loving—so Christlike—it can't help but be attractive to most people.

In one of his most popular books, *Improving Your Serve*, Chuck Swindoll suggests that as we serve others we become like stars to a darkened world.[8] Oh, I love that analogy—and because we don't have streetlights, stars are a big part of my nighttime world. Their sparkling beauty makes it easy to think of them as graceful beacons lighting up the nighttime sky.

It's *His* Light That Makes the Difference

I've saved the most important part of this chapter until last. Let me begin by telling you what I found last week tucked away with some keepsakes.

Every so often I sort through one of the boxes in the garage. These aren't your ordinary boxes. Some of them have traveled from California to Oregon and now to Arizona. When they were first packed, I wrote "SAVE" in big red letters across the front of each. Right below my handwriting, Al added "sort before next move"—with an exclamation mark.

That was four moves ago.

Last week I peeled the brittle-but-still-holding masking tape off one of the final four boxes. About a third of the way down, nestled in with school reports, birthday cards, and a collection of Hallmark paper dolls, I found the top sheet of an old church bulletin. It was from Village Church in Burbank, California.

I know why I saved it. The picture and the Bible verse represent the difference that took place in my life when I asked Jesus into my heart almost forty years ago.

The verse on the front of the bulletin is Psalm 27:1: "The LORD is my light and my salvation." The words *Lord, light,* and *salvation* are in a different color from the rest of the words, and they are about five times bigger. Behind the words is a hill overlooking the ocean. A white lighthouse stands high on the hill, with a single beacon breaking through the darkness.

That's what Jesus did for me. He broke through my darkness. And that's what He does for every person who receives Him as Savior. If we have any light at all, it is because He scatters the darkness of our hearts and allows His beauty to be illumined through us.

In *Mirror, Mirror: What Is My Heart Reflecting*, my friend Marilyn McAuley drew a lovely picture of how this happens:

When I was a Girl Scout in grade school, the Girl Scout Council of our city staged an annual lantern parade. Every Girl Scout in the city created a lantern that would be judged for originality and beauty.

At sundown, we lit our lanterns and lined up to parade before the townspeople. We walked up one side of the boulevard and down the other in single file so the delicate patterns could best be seen. People lined the street to watch as the lit lanterns displayed the unique artwork of each girl. The lanterns were just so much cardboard, cellophane, and paint until the flashlights were turned on inside. Then the beautiful patterns of each lantern were revealed. No longer did we see the cardboard and paint, only the lovely colors of the cellophaned designs illumined.[9]

And so it is with each of us. We're just like so much cardboard and paint until the One called "The Light of the World" comes in and lights up our lives.

And once He does, we get to be part of His irresistible light parade.

A Cinderella Story

This chapter started with a Disney light parade and now ends with a Disney princess. But as you will see, the story is so much more than that. In his winning style, preacher and writer Max Lucado needs only a few well-crafted words to present a powerful message.

I received a call from a friend named Kenny. He and his family had just returned from Disney World. "I saw a sight I'll never forget," he said. "I want you to know about it."

He and his family were inside Cinderella's castle. It was packed with kids and parents. Suddenly all the children rushed to one side. Had it been a boat, the castle would have tipped over. Cinderella had entered.

Cinderella. The pristine princess. Kenny said she was perfectly typecast. A gorgeous young girl with each hair in place, flawless skin, and a beaming smile. She stood waist-deep in a garden of kids, each wanting to touch and be touched.

For some reason Kenny turned and looked toward the other side of the castle. It was now vacant except for a boy maybe seven or eight years old. His age was hard to determine because of the disfigurement of his body. Dwarfed in height, face deformed, he stood watching quietly and wistfully, holding the hand of an older brother.

Don't you know what he wanted? He wanted to be with the children. He longed to be in the middle of the kids reaching for Cinderella, calling her name. But can't you feel his fear; fear of yet another rejection? Fear of being taunted again, mocked again?

Don't you wish Cinderella would go to him? Guess what? She did!

She noticed the little boy. She immediately began walking in his direction. Politely but firmly inching through the crowd of children, she finally broke free. She walked quickly across the floor, knelt at eye level with the stunned little boy, and placed a kiss on his face.

"I thought you would appreciate the story," Kenny told me. I did. It reminded me of another one. The names are different, but isn't the story almost the same? Rather than a princess of Disney, it's the Prince of Peace. Rather than a boy in a castle, it's a thief on a cross. In both cases a gift was given. In both cases love was shared. In both cases the lovely one performed a gesture beyond words.

But Jesus did more than Cinderella. Oh, so much more.

Cinderella gave only a kiss. When she stood to leave, she took her beauty with her. The boy was still deformed. What if Cinderella had done what Jesus did? What if she assumed his state? What if she had somehow given him her beauty and taken on his disfigurement?

That's what Jesus did.

"He took our suffering on him and felt our pain for us.

. . . He was wounded for the wrong we did; he was crushed for the evil we did. The punishment, which made us well, was given to him, and we are healed because of his wounds."[10]

Make no mistake.

Jesus gave more than a kiss—he gave his beauty.

He paid more than a visit—he paid for our mistakes.

He took more than a minute—he took away our sin.

MAX LUCADO
From *A Gentle Thunder*[11]

A Gentle Touch
For discussion or journaling

*For God, who said, "Let there be light in the
darkness," has made us understand that this
light is the brightness of the glory of God
that is seen in the face of Jesus Christ.*

2 Corinthians 4:6[12]

1. What type of light are you—candle, lighthouse, match, bare light bulb, flashlight turned on and off, oil lamp? Explain why you consider yourself to be this kind of light.

2. Edith Wharton's quote on page 4 states, "There are two ways of spreading light; to be the candle or the mirror that reflects it." Explain how this quote relates to your life.

3. If you were trying to encourage someone who was struggling with having a regular quiet time with the Lord, what suggestions would you add to the list on pages 7 and 8?

A Prayer from the Heart

Dear Lord,

It's hard to imagine You describing me as the light of the world. That is Your name. It would seem more fitting if You just called me one of the twinkling lights in the parade—and there are plenty of days when I feel that I don't even do that very well. Please help me shine more brightly so that someone will be able to find his or her way out of the darkness. ♡

CHAPTER 2

When Daisies Dance

I wonder what the wind whispers to the daisies—
making them ruffle and twirl about?
My heart smiles just thinking about it!

KIMBER ANNIE ENGSTROM

When I picked up the mail that afternoon, the envelope with daisies dancing around its border immediately caught my attention. The cheerful blooms with their familiar white petals and bright yellow centers looked like a scrap of happiness poking through the stack of bills and junk mail.

Although I didn't recognize the name on the return address, something about the delicate penmanship intrigued me. Carrying the letter in to the living room, I sank down into the sofa and propped my feet up on the coffee table. The two-page letter began with these words: "Dear Alice . . . You won't remember me, but I was at the retreat where you spoke last weekend, and I just wanted to thank you for . . ."

The funny thing was, I did remember her. Something she wrote in the letter triggered my memory, and I knew it was Pat, the woman with the radiant smile who had come up after the conference and talked with me for a few minutes. I also remembered her as the woman who sat on the left side of the auditorium about five rows from the front. Pat had nodded her head in agreement at several points, laughed when I tried to be funny, and brushed tears from her cheeks during the tender moments of my talk.

Speakers look for people like Pat when they need encouragement. And now, on a day when I was feeling blue about a family situation, I received this thank you from Pat for something I had mentioned at the retreat.

I wonder if encouragers like Pat—those dear people whose words fall on our hearts like "apples of gold in settings of silver"[1]—know what a blessing they can be. I wonder if they know what a difference they make in the lives of others.

> We have a Christian duty to encourage one another. Many a time a word of praise or thanks or appreciation or cheer has kept a man on his feet. Blessed is the man who speaks such a word.
>
> WILLIAM BARCLAY

Have you had such an experience with an encourager?

Or just as important—have you embraced your opportunities to be such an encourager?

It seems that the more we mature in Christ, the more concerned we are about other people. When the Bible says, "Let each of you look out not only for his own interests, but also for the interests of others,"[2] surely this must include sharing things like hope, forgiveness, love, grace, mercy, compassion, kindness—and yes, encouragement. These are the kinds of gifts that Christ has lavished on us, and now we have the opportunity to pass them on to the people we encounter in our everyday lives.

THE GIFT OF ENCOURAGEMENT

I like the word encourage. When used in the New Testament, it stems from the Greek word parakaleo, which means to stand with or to come alongside. One of the meanings in Webster's dictionary is "to give support to." And my thesaurus suggests synonyms like *reassure*, *cheer*, *inspire*, *approve*, and *applaud*.

Sounds a little like being a cheerleader, doesn't it? But the truth is, there's a whole lot more to encouraging others than just waving pompoms and shouting from the sidelines.

The New International Version of the Bible uses the word *encourage* thirty-eight times in verses like:

- Hebrews 3:13: "Encourage one another daily."
- 1 Thessalonians 5:11: "Therefore encourage one another and build each other up."
- Romans 1:12: "That you and I may be mutually encouraged by each other's faith."

As I was reading through these passages, I thought about the many times other people have come alongside me and led the cheers. It seems to me that encouragement is in order in three different kinds of situations.

Sometimes it's a way to celebrate good news or positive developments in someone's life—to say, "Good for you" or "I knew you could do it" or just "Yippee!"

Sometimes it's a way of supporting others—providing help and comfort and empathy when storm clouds gather.

Sometimes it's just to brighten an ordinary day—to give a little lift and extra encouragement during those blah times.

When you think of it, those three different situations suggest a helpful outline for how we can be effective and loving encouragers.

CELEBRATING GOOD NEWS

I love confetti! And fireworks! And balloons! And parties! And cheers! Any reason at all, let's celebrate. At least, that's how I feel most of the time.

If you're like me, you may have wondered why Scripture has to *tell* us to "rejoice with those who rejoice."[3] After all, isn't it almost second nature to launch balloons and throw confetti when something good happens?

No, not always.

Did someone else get the promotion you deserved?

Did someone else win the contest? Get asked to do the solo? Get pregnant when you have waited so long?

Did someone else's son get to play while yours sat on the bench?

Did someone else's daughter win the scholarship while yours dropped out of high school?

The list could go on and on. And no, it's not always easy to rejoice when others rejoice.

One evening a beautiful young woman in her late twenties telephoned me. We had prayed for almost a year that God would provide a godly man to be her husband, but so far the prayer remained unanswered. She called to tell me that her roommate had just gotten engaged. With a little sob caught in her throat, she said, "Please pray that I will rejoice."

Three weeks later I saw this same young woman and her roommate at the stationery store—chairs side by side, heads bent over a stack of catalogs, searching for the perfect wedding invitation. When they looked up, both faces were absolutely radiant. My friend smiled and gave me a little thumbs-up sign.

When we talked again, I asked what had made the difference. She said that she had started doing little things to celebrate her roommate's happiness, and the celebratory feelings had just followed.

Oh, what a great plan! When it's hard for me to rejoice, I think about the example of this precious young woman, and it makes all the difference. There's just something about rejoicing that's contagious—even when you have to catch it from yourself.

And yes, I know it's not always that easy. To be honest, rejoicing with others can sometimes feel like a chore—or even impossible. But I can honestly say that whenever I've made the effort to look beyond my own desires and cheer for another, I have almost always (sometimes *eventually*) received the gift of encouragement for myself as well.

There's another key to celebrating with others. It's best told by a delightful story written by a woman named Marie Curling, who lives in England. The story is about what she learned from little Jamie Scott.

Jamie was trying out for a part in his school play. His mother told me that he'd set his heart on being in it, though she feared he would not be chosen. On the day the parts were awarded, I went with her to collect him after school. Jamie rushed up to her, eyes shining with pride and excitement.

"Guess what, Mum," he shouted, and then said those words that remain a lesson to me: "I've been chosen to clap and cheer."[4]

Isn't that a wonderful thought—that clapping and cheering for others might actually be something we're chosen for and called to, a "supporting" role as vital as the starring one?

WHEN STORM CLOUDS GATHER
(AND KEEP HANGING AROUND)

The same verse that says, "Rejoice with those who rejoice," also tells us to "weep with those who weep." For most of us, the longer we live—and the more of our own tears we cry— the better we appreciate what weeping with others means. It's a matter of caring, listening, and giving whatever comfort we can. Experience can help us do this, because it's in receiving comfort that we best learn to comfort others.

But learning to weep with those who are weeping involves more than just accumulating heartaches—there are plenty of hurting people who *haven't* learned to reach out to others. Encouraging others in dark times requires empathy and imagination—as well as a heart that is open to the Spirit's nudging.

For most of my young life, I was pretty insensitive to people who were hurting. Because I didn't know what to say, I either avoided them altogether or I said something that didn't seem to help at all. Then, one day when I was doing my morning devotions, a verse from Hebrews 13:3 seemed to jump off the page. It turned a light on for me. The verse says, "Remember the prisoners as if chained with them."

Do you see it, too? We are to remember the person as though the sorrow were our own. From that day forward, I found myself asking: *If this were happening to me, what would bring me the most comfort? What would I want to hear? What would I want others to do? What would help the most?*

I know there were still times after that when I said or did the wrong thing, but that verse helped me become a little less me-centered and a lot more sensitive to the needs of others.

Another thing I've learned about weeping with others is that many needs are long-term and ongoing, and that our offers of love and encouragement need to be long-term as well. I think Christians as a whole are pretty good comfort givers when difficulties first hit. When someone loses a job, when a husband leaves, when a friend first discovers drugs in her son's bedroom or finds out her teenage daughter is pregnant, when a neighbor is diagnosed with cancer, when a loved one dies, we are right there with meals and visits and cards and prayers and babysitting and even financial help.

> *Lonely people, hurting people need someone to help them up. To encourage them, to support them, to let them know they're not alone.*
>
> BILLY GRAHAM

But what happens when there isn't another job? When the child becomes more and more rebellious, when the husband doesn't come back home, when the cancer spreads? When the storm clouds linger and the hard times stretch into months and even years. Where are the cheerleaders then? Where are those who are willing to come alongside with loving encouragement?

I once attended a grief recovery seminar where a young widow shared her story. Her husband had died in an accident, leaving her to raise two young children on her own. She spoke about all the wonderful things people did at the beginning of her grief. But then, after about six months, when she was still hurting, it was as though everyone else had forgotten. She longed to hear people say her husband's name or talk about the things they use to do together as a couple. But no one said a word. She hoped that some of the men from church would take her son fishing as they had promised. But no one called. At night when she had trouble sleeping, she wondered if anyone still prayed for her. But no one said they did.

Seeing the hint of sadness that still lingered in that woman's eyes, I thought about all the times when I had only comforted at the beginning of the sorrow. We need to find ways to let people know we still care, to follow through on what we said we would do when grief was brand-new. We need to let people know we are still praying for the prodigal child or the worsening illness or the ongoing unemployment. Meals delivered in the first weeks after someone dies are appreciated, but a meal shared together six months later means even more.

Oh, we must be very sensitive because, as Ruth Graham reminds us, on every Sunday morning, in every pew, sits someone with a broken heart.[5]

For those of you who are reading this and have no one to comfort and encourage you, I wish I could sit next to you and wrap my arms around you as others have wrapped their arms around me. Thankfully, Jesus *is* there with you—closer than the air you breathe. In His Love Letter, He has written tender promises to comfort you. Like a shepherd carries a little lamb, He will carry you close to His heart until you are strong again.[6] He may actually send another person to love you in His name. He may speak to you through the words of Scripture. Or He may simply draw close to you in silence.

I urge you to open your heart to whatever form of comfort the Lord provides for you. Then one day, when skies are bluer, you will be able to comfort others with the same comfort that you receive.[7]

On Ordinary Days

When I remember the day I found Pat's daisy-trimmed envelope in my mail, I get a happy feeling in my heart. It must be because I expect cards on my birthday and holidays, and so receiving a card or letter on an ordinary day seems even more special. Something like that can be enough to cure a case of "the blahs" and transform ordinary into wonderful.

Of course there are hundreds of ways to be an "everyday" cheerleader. But writing notes is one of my favorites, and it's something everyone can do. In our electronic age, many of us do most of our correspondence by e-mail—and an e-mail can certainly be a source of encouragement. But there is still something about a handwritten note that makes me want to put it in my box of keepsakes. I love it when I run across the notes my mother wrote me years ago. I trace my finger over her handwriting and sometimes hold the faded paper next to my heart.

Notes of encouragement don't require expensive stationery or store-bought cards. Even a recipe card with a stamp affixed to it will do. Tuck a few cards in your Bible to have handy when the Lord brings someone to mind during your devotions. Carry them in your car or purse so you can dash off a bit of encouragement while you're waiting for an appointment or happen to arrive early to pick up the kids.

> *The beauty of the written word is that it can be held close to the heart and read over and over again.*
>
> FLORENCE LITTAUER

In the following few paragraphs are seven random ideas for encouraging people through note writing. Perhaps you will find at least one that calls out to you as a real possibility:

- Children and grandchildren, nieces and nephews love getting their own mail. I suppose the little ones like it best, but no matter what their ages, fancy up the envelopes. Try stickers, hearts, glitter—anything that communicates, "You are very special." Inside, tell them something wonderful that you have noticed about them. A kindness to another child. A job well done. Help to someone in trouble. Respect for an older person.

- Teenagers live in a world of so many negatives. So maybe you can take a moment to write a few lines of encouragement to a teen—your own, someone in your church youth group, or just a kid you have noticed in the neighborhood. Chances are, there are plenty of people to point out that teen's problems, but you can point out his or her possibilities. (Even a teen with metal things hanging from nose and lips will have traits worthy of praise.) And don't be fooled by a teenager's attempt to seem blasé or "cool"— those words of praise will make a difference. Even when they are grown, they probably will remember what you wrote. Sometimes even a few words of encouragement can be like a signpost pointing someone toward his or her dreams.

> *Set a word of love heart-deep in a person's life. Nurture it with a smile and prayer and watch what happens.*
>
> MAX LUCADO

- When people blow it, they usually feel miserable. They wonder how long others will remember their mistakes and hope that they'll be given another chance. Some may even feel like giving up. At such times, a simple note can give someone the courage to keep going. I like what one mother wrote to her son, "I know things are tough right now. Life sometimes gives you the test before you've had a chance to study the lesson. I know you'll succeed. Keep on keeping on."

- I have a kind acquaintance named Nancy who likes to write notes to people from her past—even rather obscure people—recalling something they said or did that touched her heart or changed a thought. She says the responses are amazing. People love to be reassured that their lives have made a difference.

- I like what my friend Joyce told me about her little girl's Sunday school teacher. The teacher sent her a card with a stick of gum taped to it. The note said, "Even though I send cards to the other boys and girls when they miss Sunday school, here's a stick of gum to let you know how pleased I am that you are there every Sunday." Bless that dear teacher for being thoughtful enough to notice and encourage those everyday acts of faithfulness that are often overlooked.

- Speaking of teachers, on an ordinary day—not Christmas or a birthday—help your children write notes of appreciation to their teachers. If they are too young to write, ask them questions and then write the notes for them, but be sure to let the teacher know the words came from the children. This is a wonderful thing to do for grandparents, too.

- Pastors also need to hear words of praise. Often they are discouraged because they receive so many complaints—everything from the music being too soft or too loud or the temperature being too hot or too cold. Next Sunday afternoon, make the time to write your pastor a note. Don't just say you think he is wonderful. Telling him how you plan to use his message in your life will bless his socks off!

A LITTLE NUDGE

In all of these situations, it's important to remember we're not on our own when it comes to encouragement. We can trust God to bring to our minds people who could use an encouraging word or action. But it's up to us to act on those little "nudges" and obey.

The Lord nudged me just this week when I saw a shocking picture in our newspaper of a man who weighs 625 pounds. The accompanying article said that the last time he was able to stand on his feet was seven years ago. But he has lost 155 pounds since then, and now, with a little help from his physical therapists, he is able to sit up for almost a minute. His goal is to walk again—a goal that is at least a year down the road.

As you can imagine, this man has faced a lot of humiliation—especially two months ago when firefighters had to use a whale sling to lift him out of his house and put him on a flatbed truck to take him to the nursing home. A helicopter flew overhead taking pictures that were shown on the evening news. His response? "Don't underestimate the fat man."

I laid the paper aside, but I couldn't forget about how that man must feel. My heart just went out to him. Al and I prayed for him, but it seemed as though the Lord wanted us to do more. Since the name of the nursing home was in the paper, we were able to send him a card of encouragement. We're keeping his picture and will write again every month or so. Each time, we'll tuck a little confetti inside the envelope and tell him that we're celebrating his progress.

Isn't the world of hope, and love, and encouragement wonderful? These are some of the best gifts for receiving and even more wonderful for giving. They make your whole heart happy— like the happiness you feel when you celebrate with balloons and confetti . . . or see daisies dancing in the wind.

Beauty Contest

Over the years we might forget the names of people who have encouraged us, but we never forget the lasting impressions they leave on our hearts. The following story by Allison Harms, a freelance writer in Lake Oswego, Oregon, is about a teacher's small gift of encouragement—a gift that Allison still treasures today.

I won a beauty contest when I was in third grade. I didn't expect to. At nine years old, I already knew that my face was too full, that my eyes were set too closely together, that the angles of my chin and nose were too sharp. Besides, I wore glasses and my teeth were crooked. My body could not be called a "figure" except in geometric terms: I was a flat rectangle with a building block build. In addition to all my physical drawbacks, my older sister had informed me that I had the personality of overcooked cauliflower.

On the day of the contest, all these negative appraisals compounded my fears as I stood to be judged against a whole civilization of more beautiful girls. They had all arrived at school giggling in new dresses, shiny black patent leather shoes, curls, ribbons, even lipstick. I'm sure my dress was fine too and that my mother had done her best with my belligerently straight hair. I'd worn those pink sponge rollers overnight so at least my hair was doing something under my droopy ribbon. Still, I felt like I was facing a firing squad as the other classes filed in to watch the spectacle, laughing and pointing.

When the teacher began to list the names of the contestants, I concentrated on trying to make time fast-forward so that I could avoid this moment. I imagined being home curled up in my reading chair with my book and my cat. Drinking cocoa and eating warm cinnamon toast. Another part of my mind was already comforting my soon-to-be-rejected self. "This doesn't matter," I told myself. "The judges aren't fair. They're just going to pick the teacher's pet."

A sudden hush interrupted all the pictures and voices in my head. Then my teacher's voice, my name, and loud cheers and clapping from the crowd. A small, rough ceramic disc was placed in my hand. As I translated the words scratched into its surface, that hard, red clay became a treasure in my hand. I read: "Allison—Most Brilliant." When I raised my eyes, I saw that all the other girls held a disc too. Still giggling nervously, they began passing around their awards. Through relief-filled eyes, I read some of their happiness: each disc was inscribed with a unique message of self-worth which had been designed even before the contest had begun. There had never really been a contest! And that was the whole point.

It must have been some creative teacher's idea: to counteract that destructive third grade project of comparing ourselves to each other, to demonstrate in three dimensions that each person has beauty, gifts, abilities. That there is beauty deeper than the surface *and* beauty in our differences, not in the fact that we fit into some uniform standard.

I don't pretend that I learned that lesson once and for all that day, but it was an ordeal-turned-episode to build on. And today, when I rediscovered a small ceramic disc under some papers at the back of a drawer, I felt my face shine with the happy surprise of finding myself valued. I silently thanked the teacher whose name I have forgotten. And I smiled at the memory of an awkward nine-year-old girl who looked into the mirror that teacher held up for her and saw herself as beautiful.

ALLISON HARMS
From *Stories for the Family's Heart*[8]

A Gentle Touch
For discussion or journaling

Let's see how inventive we can be in encouraging love and helping out . . . spurring each other on, especially as we see the big Day approaching.

1. There's a poem that circled the Internet called "Lend me your hope for a while; I seem to have mislaid mine." If someone said that to you, how would you respond?

2. What's your favorite way to encourage others?

3. Think back on your own life. What teachers, relatives, and friends had a positive impact on your life? Choose one who is still living and do something to thank and encourage that person today.

A Prayer from the Heart

Dear Lord,

Ever since I was a little girl, I wanted to wave pom-poms, and now You have chosen me to be on Your cheerleading squad. No tryouts or competition or synchronized dance steps—You only ask that I humble my heart before You, pray, and then unwrap Your gifts and give them away. Thank You for choosing me to do this. Yes, thank You. ♡

CHAPTER 3

Day Brighteners

*Pretend you're a star
and poke a hole in someone's darkness.*

AUTHOR UNKNOWN

I wonder if you enjoy watching people as much as I do. To linger over coffee at a restaurant and just observe is one of my favorite pastimes. And I have found it's quite remarkable how many people I catch in the act of saying or doing something kind.

A woman stops at a table where an older couple is eating. "Excuse me," she asks, "are the two of you married?"

"Why, yes we are. Fifty-two years next month."

"That's wonderful. Congratulations!" And before turning away she adds, "I just wanted to stop and say what an attractive couple you are. It's obvious that you're still very much in love."

Before heading out the door, the same woman stops at another table where a family with three young children is finishing their meal. She smiles and says to the parents, "I've been noticing how well behaved your children are. You must be very proud of them." And then she glides out the door, leaving a trail of sunshine behind her.

On another day a group of young adults—perhaps college age, maybe older—are having breakfast. One of the girls says to the waitress, "We're about to thank the Lord for our meal, and we're wondering if there is anything we can pray about for you."

"Oh, I don't think so, but how very nice of you to ask." Is

it just my imagination, or does the waitress brush a tear from her cheek as she hurries to the next table?

I'm at an airport restaurant. A marine sits across from me, alone, almost finished with his meal. A couple, about the age his parents might be, stops and visits with him for a while. Where is he stationed? they ask. Where is he headed? How long has it been since he's been home? Before leaving, the gentleman tells the marine he would consider it an honor if he could pick up his dinner tab. He shakes the marine's hand and thanks him for serving our country. And just when I think the woman is going to lean down and give the marine a hug, he stands up instead.

The next moment is like a Norman Rockwell painting. The marine is tall, the woman petite. He stoops to give her a hug. Arms around each other, she is patting his shoulder as any mother would do to comfort her son.

Just everyday happenings, but the moments are magical.

It's hard to realize that little gestures can make much of a difference in people's lives. But I imagine that if we were to ask the elderly couple or the waitress or the marine, they would tell us such things really do matter. There's something about an unexpected kindness in our not-too-kind world that brightens a day and pokes a hole in the darkness.

Sometimes making a difference in our world calls for noble decisions and big gestures. Sometimes it requires significant sacrifices and changes in life direction. But just as often, I think, following God's heart is simply a matter of noticing another person's need and making a little effort to lift up or encourage that person. Even the smallest of these acts of grace can make a huge difference. And anyone can do it—including you and me.

This chapter is filled with ideas for sprinkling a little sunshine on others—thoughtful, wonderful, fun things to do. As you will see, they don't take much time. They just require slowing down enough to be aware of the people around you and then responding to them with love and grace—in your words, in your touch, and with your actions.

The best thing about these kinds of day brighteners is that they don't just light up other people's lives; they light up our own as well. That must be why Jesus said, "You're far happier giving than getting."[1] It's hard to sprinkle sunshine on others without getting some on yourself.

Day Brightener Ideas

- *Take flowers to the hospital and ask the nurse to deliver them to a patient who doesn't have any.*
- *Offer to return the grocery cart for an elderly person or a mother with small children.*
- *Let someone cut in front of you.*
- *Give a larger tip than usual.*
- *Send a thank-you note to someone who doesn't expect it.*
- *Take blankets to a homeless shelter or an animal shelter.*
- *Send a gift anonymously.*
- *Compliment five people in an afternoon.*
- *Donate to a worthy cause.*

- *Help without being asked.*
- *Buy a bunch of daisies and pass them out to people you pass on the sidewalk.*
- *Send a valentine to a widow.*
- *Arrange to have a tip taken to the dishwasher.*
- *Make someone new feel welcome.*
- *Run an errand for someone who is sick.*
- *Let someone know you are praying for him or her.*

FROM ALICE GRAY AND STEVE STEPHENS,
THE WORN OUT WOMAN [2]

KINDNESS SPOKEN HERE

In the last chapter, we talked about encouraging people through written words. I think it's equally important to encourage people with spoken words. If we develop this as a lifestyle, I believe it will change every relationship we have.

It begins by looking for the best in others. Everyone likes to be remembered for his or her best moments, and that's something we all can do. Philippians 4:8 teaches us to think about whatever is noble, just, pure, lovely, of good report, virtuous, and praiseworthy. Applying that verse to other people can be the key to speaking kindness to others.

One home I visited had a neon-pink sign posted on the refrigerator with "7=1" written on it in bold numbers. I asked the mother what it meant, and she said she had read an article about how continual criticism can damage a family. The article stated that it takes seven affirmations to cancel out one criticism. The sign on the refrigerator was to remind the whole family that "kindness is spoken here."

Wouldn't it be great if we all had that reminder posted on our refrigerators, office coolers, computer monitors, and rear-view mirrors, and in our day planners, and—well, you get the idea. But let's not just post it. Let's live by it.

When you are at the mall or airport or movie theater, intentionally look for the employees who sweep or pick up clutter. I like to go up to them and say, "You know, if it weren't for you, I wouldn't like coming here." Pausing just long enough for them to think I'm a bit odd, I add, "Thanks for keeping this place so clean. You're doing a great job, and I just wanted you to know how much I appreciate you."

I have wept in the night
For the shortness of sight
That to somebody's need
made me blind;
But I never have yet
Felt a tinge of regret
For being a little too
kind.

—AUTHOR UNKNOWN

Their expressions inevitably change when I do that. Their shoulders straighten a bit, and I get to walk away with a bounce in my step because I've found a way to brighten their day.

TOUCH WITH LOVE

Touching was an important part of Christ's ministry. He touched the eyes of the blind man, He blessed the children by laying His hands on them, He washed the disciples' feet. But perhaps his most stunning use of touch was when He laid hands on a man who had leprosy.[3] In Bible times, no one touched lepers. They lived outside the towns and were required to cry out "unclean" when other people came near. Not even spouses or parents or children touched a leper. When the leper asked Jesus if He would heal him, Jesus easily could have just said, "Be healed." But He didn't. Because Jesus knew how much it would mean to the man, Jesus stretched out His hand and *touched* him. I'm always moved when I read those words.

I suppose we seldom think about physical touch making a difference in people's lives. However, researchers have found that a loving, gentle touch can have profound benefits not only for children, but for people of all ages.

My friend Marilyn learned this when she started volunteering to help the homeless at a drop-in center. One of her first jobs at the center was to serve coffee, and she tried hard to make a connection with the street people. She smiled and spoke cheerfully to them, but she never felt that she was really getting through. Then one day, when she served coffee to a woman named Margaret, Marilyn reached out and gently touched the woman's hand. Margaret lifted her head, looked into Marilyn's face for the first time, and saw kindness there. It was Marilyn's loving touch that broke down the barrier.

In the practical and helpful book, *How to Really Love Your Teenager*,[4] Dr. Ross Campbell suggests that lovingly touching your teen while saying "I love you" seems to double the impact of the words. Pat a back, gently brush a cheek, hold a hand, and you might be surprised how much more your words mean.

Of course, the power of a loving touch isn't limited to children and teens. My mother, who had been a widow for more than twenty years, lived with us during the last two years before she died. (What a sweet time!) Our older son, well over six feet tall, looked like a giant next to her. His big hands were calloused and rough; hers were small and soft and parchment thin. Yet whenever Bob came to visit, the first thing he would do is sit down on the couch next to Gram Grams and hold her hand. My mother said it was the dearest thing he could do.

Oh, my. There are so many stories about how a caring touch communicates love. One of my most treasured is about a man in a nursing home. He did not remember any of his children or even his wife, though she visited every day. The family did everything they could think of to help him. They showed him photo albums and mementos of special vacations and anniversaries. They even took their collie for a visit. The response was always the same blank stare.

> *Too often we underestimate the power of a touch, a smile, a kind word, a listening ear, an honest compliment, or the smallest act of caring, all of which have the potential to turn a life around.*
>
> LEO BUSCAGLIA

Then one day his wife sat beside him. She lifted his two hands and held them in hers.

"Who am I, dear?" she asked.

The same blank stare. And then his face brightened as he looked at her hands holding his. For a moment, a familiar smile crossed his face as he said three words, "You love me."

If a loving touch has so much power, then maybe we can all find more ways to hold hands with one another.

Helping Hands

Scripture says that we are to "bear one another's burdens."[5] And sometimes, I think, this applies quite literally. We sprinkle sunshine in people's lives when we reach out to offer them a helping hand in thoughtful and practical ways.

Sometimes this is a matter of simple courtesy—holding the door for the person behind you, picking up an item someone has dropped, helping up a child who has run too fast and fallen splat on the pavement. When we choose to stop, notice, and help instead of just walking on, we are making a tangible choice to care and connect.

Earlier this week, at the grocery store, I overheard a teenager trying to get directions to a hardware store—he needed a bicycle part. No one seemed to know the nearest store, so it was a simple thing for me to pick up my cell phone and call my husband for directions. The young man couldn't get over the fact that I had taken the time to help him. "Most people wouldn't have cared," he said. It seemed sad to me that he had this general perception of people—and I think he was partly wrong. Most people *do* care—but often we're in such a hurry that we barely notice the people around us, so we miss an opportunity to sprinkle a little sunshine on our world.

Sometimes helping involves a little more effort—raking an elderly person's leaves, covering a teenager's chores to give him or her a day off, running errands for a busy friend, or folding and stacking clothes that have been left in the apartment dryer rather than just piling them on top.

However you choose to help—don't forget to reach out to family and friends as well as strangers. It can be fun to brighten a stranger's day—but even more rewarding to offer a helping hand to someone you love.

Every Once in a While

Sometimes it may seem as if your ordinary, everyday acts of kindness make no difference at all. But don't let that discourage you. When you get to heaven and find out "the rest of the story," you may be surprised to discover how many people you encouraged with your kind words, your loving touch, your helping hands. So even if you don't see the outcome now, keep showing love and compassion anyway, because that's a significant part of following God's heart.

Quite often, of course, the results are obvious—we can enjoy seeing the positive results of our words and our touch and our actions. And every once in a while, if we keep listening to God, we'll have the privilege of participating in one of His special acts of mercy and grace. My heart is still smiling, in fact, about something that happened several years ago.

I like fresh flowers but don't have a garden, so I enjoy picking up bouquets at the grocery store. A bunch of mixed flowers costs less than five dollars where I shop, and they stay fresh for more than a week. It's a treat I like to give myself.

One Friday when I was choosing my bouquet, I felt a little tap on my heart that seemed to say, *buy two*. It was just a feeling, one I could easily ignore. But I chose a second bouquet anyway and took it to the checkout line.

I pulled my cart in behind an elderly woman. She was quite small, very tidy, and seemed quite organized about her purchases. As the clerk finished bagging her few items, I felt a second nudge on my heart: *The flowers are for her*. She was already walking away, and so I grabbed one of the bouquets, told the clerk to ring me up for two, and said I'd be back in a second.

Coming up from behind, I spoke softly. "Excuse me, but I think God wants you to have these flowers." When she turned around, her wrinkled face was a wonder—tears gathering in the deep creases of her smile.

"Oh, my, I don't know what to say," she stammered. "What a lovely gift. My husband always used to bring me flowers, but I haven't had any since he died more than four years ago. Today is our anniversary, and I was feeling a bit lonely. You'll never know how much this means to me."[6]

I'll always remember that moment when God let me be part of His plan to change the world through love. All it took was a little awareness, a little obedience, a small act of grace.

And I still like buying two bouquets and listening for a little tap on my heart that says, *The flowers are for her.*

Ivy's Cookies

In the following story by Candy Abbott, you'll read about two teenage girls who delivered some homemade chocolate-chip cookies. Is it possible that something that simple could make a difference? You'll love the answer.

The clank of the metal door and the echo of their footsteps rang in the ears of Ivy and Joanne as they walked down the dingy corridor behind the prison guard toward the "big room." The aroma of Ivy's homemade chocolate chip cookies wasn't enough to override the stench of ammonia from the recently mopped floor or the bitterness and anger that hung in the air. Women's Correctional Institute was not the kind of place where seventeen-year-olds go for an outing, but Ivy had a mission.

She didn't know what she was getting into, but she had to try. With trembling fingers, she dialed the number for an appointment at the prison. Warden Baylor was receptive to Ivy's desire to visit and referred her to Joanne, another teen who had expressed interest.

"How do we do this?" Ivy asked.

"Who knows? Maybe homemade cookies would break the ice," Joanne suggested.

So they baked their cookies and here they were, bearing gifts to strangers.

"I put almonds in these," Ivy rambled nervously as they moved along. "The dough was gummier than usual . . ."

"Don't chatter," the guard snapped. "It gets the prisoners riled."

The harsh words made Ivy jump and her heart pound. She walked the rest of the distance in silence.

"Okay. Here we are," the guard grunted, keys rattling. "You go in. I'll lock the door behind you. Be careful what you say. They have a way of using your words against you. You have fifteen minutes."

Ivy noted the prisoners' orange jumpsuits and felt over-dressed. *Maybe we shouldn't have worn heels,* she thought. *They probably think we're snobs.*

Remembering the guard's admonition, the girls put the cookies on the table next to plastic cups of juice without saying a word. Some prisoners leaned against the wall; others stood around—watching. Studying. Thinking. Staring. Nobody talked. Ivy smiled at one of the women, and she scowled back. From then on, she avoided eye contact. After five minutes of strained silence, Joanne whispered, "Let's move away from the table. Maybe they'll come over."

As they stepped back, one of the prisoners blurted out, "I'm gettin' a cookie." The others followed and began helping themselves. Soon they heard the rattle of keys. Time was up.

"What a relief to get outta there," Joanne sighed as a gust of fresh air caressed their perspiring faces.

"Yeah," Ivy agreed. "But there's a tug inside me that says

we're not done. Would you be willing to go back?"

Joanne nodded with a half-smile. "How about Thursday after school?"

Week after week they came. And week after week the prisoners ate the cookies, drank the juice, and stood around in silence. Gradually, antagonistic looks were replaced by an occasional smile. Still, Ivy couldn't bring herself to speak—not a word.

Then one Thursday, an evangelist walked in. Her step was sure, her chin was high, and she glowed with the love of God. But she meant business. "I've come to pray with you," she announced. "Let's make a circle."

Ivy was awed by the inmates' compliance. Only a few resisted. Others, although murmuring, inched their way toward the middle of the room and formed a lopsided circle, looking suspiciously at one another.

"Join hands," the evangelist instructed. "It's not gonna hurt ya, and it'll mean more if you do." Slowly they clasped hands, some grasping hard, others barely touching. "Now, bow your heads." Except for the orange outfits, it could have been a church meeting.

"Okay. We're gonna pray," she continued, "and prayer is just like talking, only to God. I want to hear you tell the Lord one thing you're thankful for. Just speak it out. Don't hold back."

Ivy's palms were sweaty. I can't pray out loud, Lord. I can't even talk to these women. Guess I should set an example, but they probably don't even like me—think I'm better than them 'cause of my clothes.

The words of an inmate jolted her from her thoughts.

"I'm thankful, God, for Miss Ivy bringing us cookies every week."

Another voice compounded the shock. "God, thanks for bringing a black lady to come see us, not just Quakers and Presbyterians."

Ivy's eyes brimmed with tears as she heard, "Thank you, God, for these two ladies givin' their time every week even though we can't do nothin' to pay 'em back."

One by one, every inmate in the circle thanked God for Ivy and Joanne. Then Joanne managed to utter a prayer of gratitude for the prisoners' words. But when it came Ivy's turn, she was too choked up to speak. Her eyes burned in humble remorse over how wrong she'd been about these women. She wished she could blow her nose, but the inmates were squeezing her hands so tightly, she resorted to loud sniffles and an occasional drip.

The following week, Ivy and Joanne returned, bright-eyed, to find the prisoners talkative.

"Why do you bring us cookies every week?" a husky voice inquired from the corner of the room. When Ivy explained, she inched a few steps closer. "Can you get me a Bible?" she asked. Others wanted to know more about the Jesus who inspires teenagers to visit prisoners.

A ministry was born from Ivy's cookies. What started as a silent act of kindness and obedience turned into a weekly Bible study at the prison, which eventually grew so big it split into several groups that continue to this day. After Joanne married and moved away, Ivy continued to minister to the inmates for years. Eventually, Prison Fellowship picked up the baton.

Ivy is a grandmom now. Her radiance has increased over the years, and she brightens any room she enters. But last Thursday afternoon she indulged herself in a good cry. Curled up on the couch, wrapped in the afghan her daughter had made, she wept. Deep sobs racked her body as she remembered it had been one year since her daughter died of asthma. She ached over the loss and felt, for the first time, the full weight of her words, "The kids can live with me." The baby was asleep in his crib and the two girls were in school when the doorbell rang.

There stood a young woman, probably seventeen, with a plate of homemade cookies.

"Are you Ivy Jones?" she asked.

"Yes," she answered, dabbing her eyes with a wadded tissue.

"These are for you," the girl said as she handed the cookies to her with a shy, sad smile, turning to leave without another word.

"Thank you," Ivy whispered in a daze. The girl was halfway down the sidewalk when Ivy called out, "But why?"

"My grandmother gave me her Bible before she died last week, and her last words were, 'Find Ivy Jones and take her some homemade cookies.'"

As the girl walked away, a wave of precious memories, uncertainties, and younger days flooded Ivy's soul. Swallowing the lump in her throat, she choked back a sob and headed toward the phone. *It's been a long time since I talked with Joanne.*

CANDY ABBOTT
From *Chicken Soup for the Prisoner's Soul* [7]

A GENTLE TOUCH
For discussion or journaling

The fruit of the Spirit is love, joy,
peace, longsuffering, kindness, goodness,
faithfulness, gentleness, self-control.

GALATIANS 5:22–23

1. In the above verse, is there any "fruit" listed that is developed through *getting,* or is it all developed through *giving?* Write a few sentences to explain your answer.

2. Describe a time when someone brightened your day with a kind word, a loving touch, or a thoughtful act.

3. Read the list of day brighteners on pages 45 and 46. Choose two or three that you will do sometime this week. Why did you choose the ones you did?

A Prayer from the Heart

Dear Lord,

I can speak words of encouragement or hold some-one's hand or let someone know I'm praying for her or deliver homemade cookies—but often I don't even notice the people who might be blessed by these things. Please help me to become more aware of the people around me who need a touch of grace. Because, Lord, when *You* want to deliver a day brightener to someone, it would be an honor to be Your messenger. ♡

CHAPTER 4

Once Upon a Front Porch Swing

FRONT PORCH SWING
It tattles of spilled lemonade, it whispers of tipped teacups,
and shares of precious tears. This is a sacred place.
A place where conversation and emotion grace the air.
A place where dreams are free to dance.

KIMBER ANNIE ENGSTROM[1]

I've often dreamed of having a big, shady front porch—the kind you see in quaint towns or in magazines like *Country Living*. There always seems to be a cozy little grouping of white wicker furniture, tall glasses of strawberry lemonade, and—best of all—a front porch swing. That would be the perfect place to call up a neighbor and ask her to come over and "sit a spell."

But in reality, I've discovered that the chairs around a worn kitchen table, plastic lounge chairs in the backyard, a bench at the park, or stools at a Starbucks' counter work just as well. The important thing is to find a way to connect with your neighbors and open the gifts of hospitality, which in their own way can be instruments of grace.

WELCOME TO THE NEIGHBORHOOD

When we first moved to Eagle Crest, Oregon, ours was the first house to be built on our street. Our front porch was small—too little for a swing but big enough for a wooden bench and a wrought-iron cart that, depending on the season, held three pots of pink azaleas or red geraniums. Al and I made the best of that porch. We loved to sit outside on the bench and give a friendly wave to people as they slowed their cars to check out the neighboring brush-covered properties.

Sometimes drive-by visitors would say yes to our spontaneous invitation to come inside for a cold soda. We had such a good time promoting the benefits of our little community that the developer nicknamed us the "welcome-wagon couple."

As lots were cleared, concrete was poured, and new houses were framed and painted, we continued to have fun welcoming our soon-to-be neighbors. We even took pictures of the various construction stages for those who lived too far away to watch the daily changes.

Then, on the first morning after the moving trucks drove away, we liked to prepare a tray with a basket of fresh-baked muffins and a carafe of coffee and condiments. Usually we delivered the goodies with just a quick, "Hi, welcome to the neighborhood; we'll get together later." Then we met Mike and Kathi, a couple who *really* knew about neighborhood hospitality—and reminded us that hospitality works both ways. Even though Kathi had a towel wrapped around her head turban-style (she was in the middle of washing her hair when the doorbell rang), they asked us to come inside. For almost two hours we sat in their almost-unpacked living room, talking like the best of friends and enjoying the coffee and muffins *together.*

We only lived in that neighborhood three years. But everywhere we have lived before and after, we've enjoyed sharing neighborhood hospitality. In fact, one of the reasons we believe it's important to welcome new families is that we've moved a lot and know how much it means to be on the receiving end of warm hospitality. When we moved to our current home in Arizona, for instance, our neighbors "Bones" and Kim were our "welcome-wagon couple" and hosted a backyard barbeque so we could meet all the neighbors.

And I still chuckle when I think of Steve, only eight years old, who rang our doorbell two days after we moved to Gladstone, Oregon, many years earlier. Steve's whole face was smiling when I opened the door. "We live around the corner," he announced, "and my mom and dad want to meet you. In fact, they would really like it if you came over right now."

I had dinner cooking on the stove, but I wasn't about to miss a chance to meet the neighbors. I turned off the burners and called Al and our two sons in from the garage, and we all went packing to Steve's house. Taking us in through the back door, Steve hollered, "Mom, the new neighbors are here."

As it turned out, his parents weren't expecting us at all, but that didn't seem to matter one bit. We were immediately embraced by some of the warmest hospitality we have ever known. The unpacked boxes, half-cooked dinner, and feelings of homesickness were all forgotten as this dear family opened their hearts and welcomed us to their neighborhood.

If you haven't discovered any friendly people living on your block or in your apartment complex, maybe you can be that person. Perhaps this is how God wants to use you to make a difference in your neighborhood. The list on pages 66–67—prepared by my dear friend Barbara Baumgardner— might give you a few ideas. If you feel the Lord tugging at your heart, why not choose a couple of ideas that you are willing to try when someone new moves in. (A few of these work pretty well for long-time neighbors, too.)

10 Ways to Welcome New Neighbors

1. Acknowledge that you see them moving in, whether with a wave of your hand or a quick, "Welcome to the neighborhood. I'm looking forward to getting to know you."

2. A plate of cookies or a pot of stew can be most appreciated at their front door, but don't go inside unless invited. Then stay only a few minutes unless your offer of help is accepted.

3. When you finish with it, leave your copy of the local newspaper in their box or on their porch for the first week.

4. If the new neighbors are from out of town, a packet made up of a city map and a list of local events, museums, concerts, etc. might be really welcome. Or, with their permission, give their name and address to a local welcoming service.

5. Pick a bouquet of flowers from your garden (or the grocery store!), tie them with a pretty ribbon, and take them over.

6. Draw a simple chart with house or apartment numbers of a few close neighbors. Add the first names of the family members—including children and pets. Put your phone number next to your name with a note to call if you can help in some way.

7. Tell neighbors to let you know if they need recommendations for shopping, a dentist, dry cleaners, etc. rather than just volunteering them.

8. Never be critical of the people who used to live in your new neighbors' house or apartment.

9. After two weeks, a neighborhood dessert or potluck dinner can introduce newcomers to other people who live nearby.

10. If your offer of help or friendship is refused, don't push. Wait until your neighbors have time to get settled and look *you* over. In the meantime, smile.[2]

For a fun warm-weather idea for new neighbors, consider a gift of a picnic. Cheri Fuller describes such an arrangement in her book *The Fragrance of Kindness.*

> After church one Sunday, an elderly couple handed Maureen a colorful blanket, a full picnic basket, and a map with directions to an unknown destination.
>
> Maureen and her family followed the map to a wildflower meadow ablaze with color: red poppies, yellow coreopsis, purple irises, wild daises, and all kinds of native flora. . . . For many years after that Sunday, the family returned to the wildflowers meadow—a fragrant reminder of the gift of kindness.[3]

Getting to know your neighbors means so much more than just waving or borrowing tools. Once you begin showing an interest and caring about each other—once you really connect

—you'll feel like you really belong. And that's true no matter how long you've lived on the block.

MAKING ROOM

I remember complaining to my sister, Nola (my favorite spiritual mentor), about how hard I found it to follow the biblical commandment to "love . . . your neighbor"[4] I wanted to do more than just wave and smile at my neighbors, but there didn't seem to be any extra time. Al was working a second job as a baseball umpire, our whole family was involved at church, I had a part-time job, we volunteered at a ton of school activities, our kids were active in sports, and we already had a favorite circle of friends.

Nola didn't lecture me about being overcommitted, although she certainly could have. Instead, she gave me two pieces of wisdom that I've never forgotten:

1. You have to create space in your heart and on your calendar for your neighbors.
2. Don't try to impress them—just make "togetherness" your purpose.

We followed her advice. We began praying that the Lord would give us a genuine heart's desire to reach out to families who lived close by us. We also made a few changes to loosen up our schedule. Al gladly gave up umpiring, and we cut back a little on some of our church, school, and sports activities. We were still plenty involved and supportive, but it was amazing how even a few intentional changes gave us room not only to breathe (and sleep!), but also to notice and begin caring about our neighbors.

One of the first get-togethers we planned was a simple evening Christmas dessert for just the adults who lived on both sides of our short street—ten houses in all, counting ours. (Christmas is a good time to have neighbors over, because your house is so cozy with holiday trim.)

We sent out invitations two weeks in advance, requesting RSVPs, and we prayed every night for the couples who would come. Remembering that we wanted to make togetherness our purpose, we kept the refreshments simple.

At six o'clock, one hour before our neighbors were to arrive, we hadn't received a single reply to our invitations. We were heartbroken and discouraged—thinking for sure that no one on the block liked us. Nevertheless, just in case someone came, we turned on soft Christmas music, lit pine-scented candles, and waited. At ten minutes after seven, the doorbell rang—it was our neighbors right across the street from us. In the following few minutes, the doorbell rang eight more times! Everyone came. Most had never been inside another neighbor's home, and some had never met even though they lived on the same block.

We played a simple getting-to-know-you game where we found out about favorite hobbies, best vacations, how long each of us had lived in the neighborhood, and what brought us here. In no time our home was filled with newfound friends and laughter.

Our neighborhood hospitality efforts became easier after that. No more cards with RSVPs. Instead, we made simple telephone calls or went door-to-door inviting neighbors for Saturday morning coffee, backyard barbeques, progressive dinners, block-wide garage sales, relaxing Bible studies, homemade ice cream for all the kids, reading groups, invitations to church, and morning walks. Best of all, soon those same neighbors were calling us to say, "Hey, I just pulled cinnamon rolls out of the oven. Can you and Al come over for a cup of coffee?"

"You bet. We'll be right over."

THE GIFT OF HOSPITALITY

Hospitality, of course, involves much more than just your physical neighbors. The Bible makes it clear that God wants all of us to make welcoming others into our homes a part of our everyday lives.[5] The *Life Application Study Bible* explains, "Some people say they cannot be hospitable because their homes are not large enough or nice enough. But even if you have no more than a table and two chairs in a rented room, there are people who would be grateful to spend time in your home."[6]

Not long ago, a young married couple asked us over to their tiny apartment for dessert. We sat at a card table they had set up in their kitchen and ate Oreo cookies and milk. (Yes, following their lead, we separated the outer wafers, licked the inside frosting, and dipped the wafers in milk.) We had a wonderful evening. This dear young couple fulfilled what I believe is the best definition of hospitality—which is simply making someone else feel comfortable.

Many people include hospitality among the spiritual gifts God gives to help us minister to one another.[7] And it's true that some people seem especially "gifted" when it comes to reaching out and welcoming others.

When Al and I were new Christians, there were two couples at our church, Rich and Barbara and Bob and Glenda, who obviously had this gift. It was as though they couldn't resist inviting people over just so they could enfold them in comfort and friendship. Sometimes it was for planned sit-down dinners, and at other times it was for a spur-of-the-moment, come-over-and-see-what's-in-the-refrigerator kind of meal. The mayor and his wife and families on welfare felt equally welcome under their umbrella of hospitality. And part of their gift was doing everything with such apparent ease.

> *Can a simple dinner party for the neighbors change the world? Yes!*
> KAREN MAINS

But what about the rest of us who don't have "the gift"— and feel overwhelmed by the prospect of opening our hearts and homes?

First, we need to realize that practicing hospitality is an important part of following God's heart. In fact, God made a special point of telling us in 1 Peter 4:9–10 to "be hospitable to one another without grumbling."

If that seems like a huge stretch for you, begin by asking God to put a genuine desire in your heart to welcome others into your home and your life. And, at the same time, ask Him to help you find the practical guidance and help you need to make this possible. Perhaps a friend or family member who feels comfortable with hospitality can come alongside and help you in your first endeavors. Or, you might prefer reading one of the following books that I like to recommend for anyone who feels a bit challenged in the hospitality department.

Jane Jarrell's *Simple Hospitality* is packed with fresh ideas presented in a light, humorous tone. This author's passion for creating an environment of love and concern is inspiring— and contagious. Another great book with delightful ideas and fifty easy recipes is *The Pleasure of Your Company* by Ann Platz and Susan Wales. This is an especially good resource for theme parties and luncheons. And one of my all-time favorite forever books is *Welcome Home* by Emilie Barnes with Anne Christian Buchanan. It's filled with phrases like "a house with a smiling face." If you are interested in creating a cozy, welcoming home, you will be helped and inspired by reading this book.[8]

A HOSPITALITY POTPOURRI

For the last few pages of this chapter, I've gathered some ideas that might help you feel more at ease in reaching out to your neighbors. If you still feel a bit intimidated, start by inviting family and friends that you already feel comfortable with and then widen the circle from there. Keep in mind that although these ideas are practical in nature, the overall message behind simple hospitality is that it is one of the pathways for sharing God's love with others.

- Invite some neighbors over for breakfast rolls and have each person bring a favorite mug or teacup. Discussing why the cup is meaningful makes a great conversation starter.
- Skip dinner and have your neighbors over for ice-cream sundaes. Set out the ice cream and a variety of toppings and let your guests craft their own creations.
- Inside or out—hang strands of white lights to brighten areas and create a soft mood.
- Have at least one toy center where children can amuse themselves while adults visit.
- Invite neighbors to an old-fashioned watermelon feed in your backyard. Ice down the melons in tin tubs, slice, and enjoy!
- Instead of cooking, consider pizza delivery or hosting a potluck where everyone brings a favorite dish.
- Entertain after sundown. That way your guests won't notice the undusted places.
- Fresh daisies in a glass jar with a checked ribbon tied around it make a charming summer centerpiece.
- Invite just one couple over and serve dinner on a card table that has been set up in front of the fireplace . . . or in the backyard under the stars . . . or on the front porch by candlelight.
- Over the years, it's been my habit to keep at least six baking potatoes in the bin, cheddar cheese in the refrigerator, and

cans of chili in the cupboard. If friends stop by unexpectedly, I ask if they want to stay for a dinner of baked potatoes with chili-and-cheese topping. Those impromptu times have made some of our best memories.

- A good idea for a winter get-together is a progressive mug party. I first heard about the idea from my friend Diane Van Wyk. In our book, *A Keepsake Christmas*, Susan Wales and I suggest holding it during the holidays because everyone's home is so festive, but it can be done anytime—just adjust the menu a little. Here's how easy it is:

Each person brings a favorite Christmas mug. (Give prizes for the biggest, prettiest, and most humorous.) At the first house, appetizers are served and the partygoers' mugs are filled with a choice of eggnog, wassail, or hot chocolate. Guests wash and dry their own mugs, then everyone heads off to the next house for salad. At the third home, guests fill their mugs with a hearty soup entrée. The last house features a yummy mug dessert consisting of a brownie and a scoop of peppermint ice cream drizzled with chocolate syrup and topped with a dollop of whipped cream. End the evening with a round of Christmas carols . . . and to all a good night![9]

My files are bursting with other ideas, but I hope these few will be enough to encourage you to have people over even if you don't have the "gift" of hospitality. Whether sitting in your front porch swing or leaning your elbows on a worn kitchen table, you can start sharing God's love with your neighbors by opening the doors of your heart and welcoming them inside.

The Spirit of Hospitality

When it comes to learning about hospitality, who can be more of an encouragement than Emilie Barnes? Gracious, kind, open heart, open home—that's how I always think of her.

The "parlor" was tiny, just an extra room behind the store. But the tablecloth was spotless, the candles were glowing, the flowers were bright, the tea was fragrant. Most of all, the smile was genuine and welcoming whenever my mother invited people to "come on back for a cup of tea."

How often I heard her say those words when I was growing up. And how little I realized the mark they would make on me.

Those were hard years after my father died, when Mama and I shared three rooms behind her little dress shop. Mama waited on the customers, did alterations, and worked on the books until late at night. I kept house—planning and shopping for meals, cooking, cleaning, doing laundry—while going to school and learning the dress business as well.

Sometimes I felt like Cinderella—work, work, work. And the little girl in me longed for a Prince Charming to carry me away to his castle. There I would preside over a grand and immaculate household, waited on hand and foot by attentive servants. I would wear gorgeous dresses and entertain kings and queens who marveled at my beauty and my wisdom and brought me lavish gifts.

But in the meantime, of course, I had work to do. And although I didn't know it, I was already receiving a gift more precious than any dream castle could be. For unlike Cinderella, I lived with a loving Mama who understood the true meaning of sharing and joy—a Mama who brightened people's lives with the spirit of hospitality.

Our customers quickly learned that Mama offered a sympathetic ear as well as elegant clothes and impeccable service. Often they ended up sharing their hurts and problems with her. And then, inevitably, would come the invitation: "Let me make you a cup of tea." She would usher our guests back to our main room, which served as a living room by day and a bedroom by night. Quickly a fresh cloth was slipped on the table, a candle lit, fresh flowers set out if possible, and the teapot heated. If we had them, she would pull out cookies or a loaf of banana bread. There was never anything fancy, but the gift of her caring warmed many a heart on a cold night. . . .

My Mama's willingness to open her life to others—to share her home, her food, and her love—was truly a royal gift. She passed it along to me, and I have the privilege of passing it on to others. What a joy to be part of the spirit of hospitality!

EMILIE BARNES
From *The Spirit of Loveliness*[10]

A GENTLE TOUCH
For discussion or journaling

Be devoted to one another in brotherly love.
Honor one another above yourselves. . . . Share with
God's people who are in need. Practice hospitality.

ROMANS 12:10, 13[11]

1. What do you think is the best way to welcome someone who is new to your neighborhood? To your workplace? To your church?

2. What have been your experiences when you were new in some of the situations listed in the above question? What can you learn from those experiences?

3. On a scale of 1–10 (1 being the lowest), how would you rate yourself in the area of hospitality? Glance over the chapter and choose one idea that will help you as you try to reach out to others.

A Prayer from My Heart

Dear Lord,

I may never have a front porch swing, but I want to have a welcoming heart. Help me to make room in my schedule for neighbors, and help me to be sensitive to people who are newcomers in other situations. Perhaps I can be the one who reaches out and invites others into a circle of warm hospitality.

CHAPTER 5

Hearts Entwined

A friend will strengthen you with her prayers,
bless you with her love,
and encourage you with her heart.

AUTHOR UNKNOWN

*I*t was Friday night, and although there were only six hundred seats, almost a hundred more women crowded into the campground auditorium. Some carried folding chairs; others sat cross-legged on the floor. All were giddy from too much coffee, rounds of hilarious laughter, and the excitement of getting away for the weekend. But it was amazing how quickly they fell into a hushed silence when the auditorium lights dimmed.

The stage was dark except for two spotlights that made perfect circles on the opposite ends of the stage floor. There were no visible props, and a simple beige curtain formed the only backdrop. Two women stood on stage, each in the center of one of the illuminated circles, facing away from each other and slightly away from the audience. Each wore all black clothing with white gloves. They stood so still, they looked like mannequins rather than real people.

From somewhere a flute began to play, and as the pure notes filled the auditorium, the two women slowly turned toward each other, revealing the masks they held in front of their faces. Taking small, somewhat hesitant steps, they began moving toward each other, heads bent down, right hands holding their masks up, left arms pressed diagonally like protective banners across their chests.

When the two women were about three feet from each other, something wonderful happened. They lifted their heads and started lowering their masks. They inched closer, the masks coming down a little with each step. Occasionally one of the women would hesitate, briefly raise her mask, but then quickly lower it again. By the time they reached center stage, the masks covered only the tips of their chins. Smiling now, each stretched one hand forward to touch the other's fingertips.

A moment later, as the flutist's notes rose to a crescendo, their masks slipped silently to the floor, and the two women embraced. The spotlights dimmed, the music faded, and the audience erupted in applause.

The title of the skit? *Friendship.*

I was at that women's camp when the two mimes performed. Later that night, in our devotional time, our cabin group discussed what it meant to *become* friends. It's true that occasionally, through a bit of serendipity, we meet someone and know almost immediately that we will be good friends. But most often, drawing close to a potential friend is more like the journey portrayed in the skit. It takes both time and courage to lower our masks enough to really embrace a friend.

LEVELS OF FRIENDSHIP

In her excellent book *Relationships: What It Takes to Be a Friend,*[1] Dr. Pamela Reeve describes three kinds of friends: acquaintances, companions, and intimate friends.

Acquaintances are the people with whom we have casual encounters—the woman behind our favorite cosmetic counter, another employee who works in the same large office complex, or a mother we sometimes talk to at our children's preschool. We recognize them, say hello, and know a little about their role in life, but that's about all. As Dr. Reeve puts it, "We know *who* they are, but it's fuzzy after that."

Companions, on the other hand, are the people we see on a more frequent basis. Perhaps we're in the same Bible study group, play golf at the same club, volunteer for the same organization, or go to the same quilting class. While stitching across the table from each other or discussing the Bible in a small circle of women, we realize that we're *connecting*. Before long we're choosing seats next to each other or signing up to serve on the same committee. Of this group, Dr. Reeve comments: "We not only know *who* they are, but *what* they are about."

Somewhere along the journey, a few companions become intimate friends. Dr. Reeve describes them like this: "We not only know *who* they are and *what* they are about . . . we know *why* and *where* they are in life." We make plans to spend more time together and look forward to the cherished hours where we can share our hearts—where we can play and work and laugh and cry and pray and hold hands through the darkest hours. When this happens, we've found what Lucy

> *Many people enter our lives for just a little while; others pause and plant flowers in our hearts that continue to bloom forever.*
>
> AUTHOR UNKNOWN

Maud Montgomery's *Anne of Green Gables* described as a "kindred spirit." And that kind of friend, I believe, is one of life's true treasures.

Perhaps the best friends are those with whom we have a history—those wonderful old friends whose fellowship and influence stretches back through the years. But even friends we've known for only a brief season can touch our hearts and change our lives. And we can do the same for them.

THE VALUE OF FRIENDS

Several years ago I read an Internet article that stated,

> A landmark UCLA study suggests friendships between women are special. They shape who we are and who we are yet to be. They soothe our tumultuous inner world, fill the emotional gaps in our marriage, and help us remember who we really are. By the way, they may do even more. . . . The famed Nurses' Health Study from Harvard Medical School found that the more friends women had, the less likely they were to develop physical impairments as they aged, and the more likely they were to be leading a joyful life.[2]

I had to smile when I read about those extensive studies. I kept thinking that the conclusions, though scientifically important, were no surprise. Most women know intuitively that friends are essential for a happy, fulfilled life . . . that friendship is one of the most loving gifts we can offer another person.

In our book *The Worn Out Woman,* Dr. Steve Stephens and I list five benefits friendships provide. Here's a quick summary:

1. *Friends provide perspective.* No matter how intelligent or capable you are, there will be days when you need some clear direction, some fresh ideas, or just a different perspective. That's what friends are for.

2. *Friends provide company.* Although connecting with friends can be an effort, your time together can be as refreshing as a barefoot walk on the beach. Good friends provide a distraction from the pressures of your day, comfort for the hurts of life, and escape from loneliness.

3. *Friends provide a place to vent.* Sometimes you need a shoulder to cry on. Other times you need a willing ear to listen to your rants and raves. Then there are times when you just feel like complaining about the injustices and annoyances that fill this world. Venting to a *trusted* friend can be a lifesaver.

4. *Friends provide accountability.* Allowing yourself to be transparent and vulnerable is a wonderful protection against temptation and naïveté. You need others to check out your thinking and to catch you when you fall and lift you back to the place where you know you should be. Remember, friends know you'll be there to do the same for them.

5. *Friends provide encouragement.* When you question your competency, value, and purpose, you need someone who will come alongside with a compliment, a hug, or just an I-believe-in-you attitude.[3]

There are probably a dozen other reasons why friends are important. But standing above the scientific studies and the counsel of carefully written books is a more fundamental reality—that friendship is God's design. He created us to need each other and to find joy in fellowship, to give and receive love and loyalty, to support one another in good times and bad, and to cheer each other on as we try to follow His heart. He even filled His Love Letter, the Bible, with friendship role models: Ruth and Naomi; David and Jonathan; Jesus and the family of Mary, Martha, and Lazarus; Jesus and His closest disciples, John, James, and Peter; the apostle Paul and Timothy. Studying these Bible friends' loyalty, sacrifice, and support for one another helps us understand more fully the extraordinary richness of true friendship.[4]

I looked at more than a hundred Bible verses trying to find a succinct verse that would explain the value of friends. There were many I could have selected, but my favorite is this beloved passage from Ecclesiastes:

Two people can accomplish more than twice as much as one. . . . If one person falls, the other can reach out and help. But people who are alone when they fall are in real trouble. . . . A person standing alone can be attacked and defeated, but two can stand back-to-back and conquer. Three are even better, for a triple-braided cord is not easily broken.[5]

Don't you love that idea of good friends being "braided" together, heart and soul? Not only is this important for individual friends—it's also important when we want to make a difference in the world, because two friends together can do far more good than either could alone.

If one or two close friends can mean this much, then shouldn't we make it a priority to find and keep friends?

FINDING FRIENDS

It seems that some women collect close friends as easily as they collect shoes, while others find it rather difficult to move through the stages from acquaintances to companions to intimate friends. Some individuals may be naturally timid, while others may be quite content with solitary pursuits like books, gardening, and painting. Some women have such exhausting schedules they have little energy left to pursue friendships, and still others might have been hurt or betrayed in a relationship and are a little shy about opening their hearts again. However, no matter what your personality or inclinations, your workload or your past experiences, I believe you'll find that developing at least a few close friendships is well worth the time and risks.

How do you start? Begin praying that God will let your path cross with others who might become your friends. Then start going to places where you might meet some kindred spirits.

For most Christians, the first place to connect is at church. It's unlikely that you will build relationships if you just attend worship services, so try to plug into some kind of small-group activity, too. If you are an at-home mom with young children, a fellowship group like MOPS (Mothers of

Preschoolers) or a daytime Bible study that offers child care might be just what you need. If you are a career woman, ask about evening events or perhaps a group that meets early in the morning before work. And because shared work is a great way to build relationships, try volunteering for the choir, an outreach project, or even a committee.

Outside of church, most communities offer myriad opportunities to spark friendships while participating in worthwhile projects. If you're interested in politics, your party probably has a local chapter. If you love the arts, seek out ways to be involved beyond attending exhibits and concerts. Check out classes and clubs for your hobbies. Discover a bookstore literary group, join a civic club, volunteer at your child's school, play in the community band, or be the person on your block who welcomes new neighbors. Truly, the possibilities are endless.

The point of all this is to put yourself in a position where you might meet someone with similar interests or values—a good starting point for friendship. But it's also good to keep an open mind about who your potential friends might turn out to be. I've found that sometimes I just "click" with people of very different backgrounds and interests and that God will occasionally put a dear friend in my life that I would never have thought to seek out.

Try not to get discouraged if friendships don't happen right away. Like the skit with the two mimes, friendship is often a slow process, but it begins by putting yourself in friendship's way. And then, if you meet someone you like, be sure to take the next step. Ask that person to share a walk or a cup of coffee or lunch. Swap phone numbers or e-mail addresses.

I remember the day Bonnie first visited our neighborhood Bible study group. New to the area, she had heard about the study when she joined the racquetball club. I liked Bonnie the moment she said hello. Right away, she explained she wasn't a churchgoer and really wasn't sure about studying the Bible, but she wanted to know if it would be okay to drop in a couple of times so she could meet other stay-at-home moms. We assured her that she would be welcome.

As it turned out, Bonnie came more than a couple of times. In fact, she attended faithfully for years. Today Bonnie is one of the most dedicated Christians I know, serving in her church and reaching out to others in her community. And wouldn't you know that some of her very best friends today are the women she met more than twenty years ago when she was new in the area and just dropped in one day at a neighborhood Bible study.

HEART-TO-HEART FRIENDS

Yesterday someone said to me, "You're the kind of friend I can call at four in the morning, and I know you will be there for me." I was so honored to hear those words—that's certainly the kind of friend I *want* to be to her. And I in turn am blessed with several friends who I could call at any time day or night.

Sometimes I wonder how certain friends have become so

dear to me. Part of the answer is that we have known each other through many seasons of life, but there is so much more that makes us sisters of the heart. As my mind drifts through the memories of so many years, I'm trying to gather the reasons into just a few words. But it's a little like wandering through a beautiful garden and trying to decide which flowers to pick for the most beautiful bouquet. How can I choose only a few?

If my dearest friends were sitting here beside me, helping me decide, I think we'd "pick" the twelve qualities listed in the sidebar on this page. These are the ways that my friends and I make a difference in each other's lives—and how we gather strength from one another to make a difference in our everyday world.

A Friendship Bouquet

- Spending time together.
- Believing in each others' dreams.
- Forgiving mistakes.
- Comforting hurts.
- Celebrating joys.
- Remembering each others' goodness.
- Telling each other the truth.
- Praying for one another.
- Protecting confidences.
- Giving and receiving.

- Keeping promises.
- Loving forever.

You might pick a very different bouquet for your best friends, of course, and it would be just as lovely as the one I would choose for mine. The important point is that enduring friendships don't just happen; they take commitment and patience and loyalty. Although there is lots of mirth and laughter, there is also sorrow and tears. But close friends stand side by side through all the many seasons of life. And when the call comes at four in the morning, they are there for each other, holding hands and drying one another's tears.

That's the simple wonder—the God-given gift—of having heart-to-heart friends.

People Need People

If you have attended a Women of Faith conference, you remember Patsy Clairmont—little in size and big in heart. As well as being a best-selling author, Patsy is a speaker who has thrilled audiences from local churches to the Pentagon. Along with presenting a clear message, Patsy has the masterful talent of moving you from warm laughter to gentle tears. That's what happened to me when I read the following story.

People need people. It's our design. . . . We will touch some lives for only moments while others we will walk with as long as there is breath in our bodies. We will work alongside comrades, play next to others, worship with many, dine with some, and live with a few folks before we depart to [heavenly] shores. . . .

Listen afresh to what Jesus asks of us: "'You shall love the Lord your God with all your heart, and with all your soul, and with all your mind, and with all your strength.' . . . 'You shall love your neighbor as yourself.'"[6] Well, I'm exhausted. "All" is everything, right? How could such a little word be packed so full? And then the Lord throws in our need to love our neighbors. Now that, girlfriend, is a full-time assignment in itself.

Actually, I've been told that I'm a full-time assignment. I

know it's true. I tend to be labor-intensive. At first it was little things like I needed help with locating my car keys. Then it grew, as I could never find my eyeglasses. Next it was my elusive purse, and more recently someone is vaporizing my car in parking lots. I seem to need more than a few people; as dingy as I am, I need an entire crew just to round up my paraphernalia. *Sigh.*

But that's truly the small stuff of life. And while we appreciate folks who are kind enough to help us get our act together, the ones who take our breath away are those who wholeheartedly show us the love of Christ when they risk coming aboard our boat in the midst of thrashing whitecaps and violent lightning strikes that threaten our very existence.

I have a darling new friend in my life. Sheila Soetaert. Sheila has been teaching me how to sail when caught in a wailing storm. She is a true-grit sailor. The gale-force winds of cancer have been threatening to capsize her vessel for some time. Sheila has learned to turn her sails until she catches the wind and allows it to be part of her momentum. She has been valiant, and many have come to help her batten down the hatches: her darling husband, her seven-year-old daughter, Chloe, other family members, her church, her support group, medical personnel, and so on. Sheila is grateful.

Recently Sheila was told that the raging seas will soon grow still and she'll be able to rest in the safety of the Lord's harbor. And as is the way of Sheila's Captain, he sent her yet another sailor to assist in this transition.

Sheila first met Annie at the hospital where Annie worked as an oncology nurse. The next time Annie and Sheila's paths crossed was at the church Sheila attended and where Annie had come to visit. Upon seeing each other again, they enjoyed, as they visited, a fast-growing friendship. Soon the two grew to be sisters of the heart. One day Annie told Sheila that when it was time for Sheila to make her way toward shore, she (Annie) would leave her job at the hospital and physically care for her.

In recent days Annie has done just that. Annie resigned her position and has climbed into Sheila's boat.

People need people.

PATSY CLAIRMONT
From *Irrepressible Hope* [7]

A GENTLE TOUCH
For discussion or journaling

A friend loves at all times.

PROVERBS 17:17

1. How would you describe a close friend to someone who had never met her? How do you think she would describe you?

2. What are some of the ways you have helped when a friend was going through a difficult time? How have you helped a friend celebrate good news?

3. In what ways do your current friendships serve as helps or hinderances to your following God's heart and offering small acts of grace to others?

4. Review the "Friendship Bouquet" on page 90. What would you add to the "bouquet of friendship"?

A Prayer from the Heart

Dear Lord,

Sometimes *lonely* can be a long word. On those days, help me remember that You are the best Friend I could ever have. No matter how wonderful other friends are, they will sometimes misunderstand or even grow distant. But You never do. As soon as I whisper Your name, I feel Your presence. You are the One above all others who comforts, protects, and always loves. Thank You for being my forever Friend. ♡

CHAPTER 6

Heartprints at Home

*Mothers—don't ever forget the permanence of your imprint.
The kids may seem ungrateful, they may act irresponsible,
they may even ignore your reminders and forget your advice.
But believe this—they cannot erase your influence.*

CHARLES R. SWINDOLL

*L*ittle Danny keeps following his mother around the house. He stays right at her heels as she cooks, makes the beds, and does the laundry. Time after time his mother encourages him to go to his room and play with his toys, but Danny doesn't want to leave.

Exasperated, his mother finally kneels down, cups Danny's chin in her hands, and asks gently, "Sweetheart, what's the matter?"

"Nothing, Mommy," he answers. Then he adds, eyes shining, "But my Sunday school teacher told us to walk in Jesus's footsteps. And since I can't see Jesus, I'm walking in yours."[1]

With few words and the sweet innocence of childhood, Danny says it best. One of the most significant roles a woman will ever have is when God entrusts her with children.

We smile when we see toddlers placing a bandage on dolly's knee, scolding teddy bears for making a mess, and kneeling beside their beds at night to pray. They are doing what Mommy does; they have been watching us even when we were unaware. And I have found that this influence doesn't end with toddlerhood or elementary school or even with the teenage years.

For all their lives, our children do more than follow our footprints. They also observe and take pictures with their hearts—images of what matters and how to live.

You could call them heartprints.

SORTING THROUGH THE PICTURES

I love taking pictures. Just ask our sons. I can still hear them saying, all through their childhood, "Oh no, here comes Mom with the camera . . . again." But I didn't care. I knew we would have good times reminiscing over all those photos. And we did, especially since I always took the time to sort out the bad shots; tossing the pictures that showed people in embarrassing poses or other unflattering situations. (I did this even before digital cameras made it easy.)

Oh, don't we wish we could do that with the pictures our children carry in their hearts? When they watch how we treat people, how we act when we are upset, how we spend money, how often we pray and read the Bible—if only they would just keep the best impressions and toss the rest.

> *If your children enter adulthood with a clear concept of who God is and what He wants them to do, you will have achieved the greatest accomplishment in life.*
>
> DR. JAMES DOBSON

Unfortunately, it doesn't work that way—at least not while children are young. They see everything, and they remember. So it's up to us to make sure our children catch us living in ways that make the best "pictures"—so that the heartprints they carry with them also reflect the image of Christ.

How do we do that? Since none of us is perfect, we'll never do it perfectly. But among the best strategies for producing beautiful heartprints are these: (1) nurturing faith, (2) teaching character, and (3) showing love.

NURTURING FAITH

Although mothers have a variety of important assignments, nothing is of higher priority than teaching their children about God's love. Everything else falls more easily in place when we have succeeded in this area.

As with everything truly significant, the task of nurturing a child's faith begins by getting on our knees and asking the Lord for wisdom. The responsibility is far too awesome to be left to chance or periodic whims.

And praying *with* our children is equally as important as praying *for* our children. If you are like me, you probably pray for your children each morning and surround them with little "arrow prayers" on and off all throughout the day. But there is nothing so dear as holding their hands and praying with them before they go off to school and kneeling with them before they fall asleep at night.

In *Lists to Live by for Every Caring Family*, Dr. Steve Stephens suggests praying for and with your children in these areas:

their health	their faith
their safety	their friends
their choices	their character
their temptations	their future mates
their contentment	their legacy[2]

Sometimes mothers ask me if I think they are overloading their children with spiritual teaching. Although each child's unique situation needs to be considered, in most cases, I answer that if parents are doing it in appealing ways, their children will probably thrive on it. The eleventh chapter of Deuteronomy commands us to teach our children while we sit at home and walk by the way, and when we lie down and rise up.[3] I think that verse means God wants us to look for every opportunity to remind our children of His love and grace.

When our four-year-old granddaughter, Summer Malu, stays the night, we have established a ritual of sitting outside in Adirondack chairs to watch the sunset. Last night the sky was spectacular with the kind of sunset that makes Arizona famous—red and purple and pink. We lingered for quite a while afterward, licking up the last drizzles of ice cream from our dishes.

"You know, Nana," Summer whispered, "God made the sunset."

"Yes, Summer," I answered, "God made the sunset. What else did God make?"

"Ice cream and lizards and . . ."

Her litany continued for another ten minutes as she named every imaginable thing known to four-year-olds. All the while I kept thinking, *With children, it is so easy to use ordinary moments to teach the extraordinary.*

In her article "Make Your Children Thirsty . . . for God,"[4] Brenda Nixon suggests some wonderful, easy ideas for teaching children about God. For instance, she wakes her daughter each morning by singing, "This is the day the LORD has made"—reminding her that each day belongs to God. While they work together in the garden to clear away leaves and debris, Brenda uses the opportunity to explain to her daughter that it is important to clear away negative attitudes and behaviors so we can flourish in our spiritual growth.

Luci Swindoll, one of the Women of Faith national speakers, often writes about the godly example of her mother. In the book *Irrepressible Hope*, Lucy writes about a daily habit of her mother's that influenced the entire family:

> The most common picture of Mother I remember is reading her Bible. She read it every day and prayed for all of us. She'd often sit in her bed and read or at the dining table where she could spread the pages open. She memorized Scripture, underlined passages, and wrote notes in the margin.[5]

It's important to recognize, though, that Luci's mother was not doing these things *just* to influence her children. Her faith was something she lived; it was part of her, and her children could see that.

Nurturing faith, in other words, is something we do first by living our own faith and second by seeking out ways to share it with our children. It's our own love of the Lord, filtered through the eyes of little ones, that will leave the clearest and most beautiful heartprints of faith.

TEACHING CHARACTER

Perhaps you've heard about the family from New York who invited a stranger to live with them. For as long as the children could remember, he had a prominent place in their home. Mom taught the children to love the Bible, and Dad taught the children to obey. But the stranger was the storyteller. His stories were so lifelike that the whole family would laugh or cry, depending on how the story was told.

Because he was like a friend, the dad didn't seem to mind that the stranger talked almost incessantly. But sometimes, while the rest of the family was enthralled with the stories, the mother would slip away and go into her room and read the Bible.

When the children got older, the storyteller got bolder. The longtime visitor started using profanity, for example, and talked as if getting high on alcohol was cool. His comments about sex were crude, and even though the kids could tell that their parents were uncomfortable with what the storyteller said, they never asked him to leave.

For all their growing up years, the stranger stayed with the family and kept telling his fascinating stories. It was only through the grace of God that the storyteller didn't influence the children more.

The storyteller's name? I'm not sure. The family just called him TV.[6]

If I were raising my kids today, one of the things I would do differently is to put restrictions on the storyteller. Doing that would leave more time for reading, more time just for playing games, more time for just hanging out together.

Some families we know have done just that. A few have taken the bold step of getting rid of television altogether. Others have become very selective in what they watch and how much time they spend watching. They also have strict guidelines about using computers.

I applaud these families. I really do. I believe the moral conditions of our times call for bold steps and strong measures. Proverbs 22:6, "Train up a child in the way he should go," leaves no doubt that God entrusts us to teach our children godly character. And that means we cannot stay on the sidelines and hope our children will turn out okay. The books we read, the music we listen to, the movies we go to, and the values we embrace in our daily habits all have a profound influence on our children.

> *Only God Himself fully appreciates the influence of a Christian mother in the molding of character in her children.*
>
> BILLY GRAHAM

One of the most powerful ways we can help our children develop a strong character is to help them develop a daily habit of reading God's Word. When they are little, you can read it to them. When they are old enough to read for themselves, encourage them to do their daily devotions at the same time you are doing yours. There are some great youth Bibles—no matter what the child's age. Instead of surprising your children with such a Bible, you might take them to a

Christian bookstore and let them pick out their own. Make a fun, relaxing time of it, and you'll create a positive, Bible-related heartprint that can help shape their lives.

There is so much more that we as parents can do to mold our children's character. Try using devotional books for dinner-table discussion, reading through a modern paraphrase of Proverbs, or enjoying Christian videos and Christian music together. (Ask your youth pastor or a staff person of your local Christian bookstore for recommendations.) Bring your children to church and encourage relationships with godly adults there. And be sure to involve children in your efforts to reach out to others. Talk to them about what you are doing and why you think it's important. Let them see you trying to follow Jesus's heart—and *snap!* Another heartprint.

> One study of middle-school girls and their mothers asked them if they talked about sexuality enough. Eighty percent of the mothers said "yes." But every single daughter said, "I wish my mother would bring it up more often." Even though parents are afraid they're not going to have any input, the fact is, our kids want to hear the truth from us.
>
> DANNAH GRESH[7]

Because of the general acceptance of premarital sex in our culture, teaching sexual purity may be one of your toughest jobs. But your children desperately need you to stay firm on this; the risks are just too high to do otherwise. When I lived in the Portland, Oregon, area, I served as director of services for five pregnancy centers that offered compassionate help to women and teens who were unprepared for pregnancy. Among those five centers, there were more than *ten thousand* client appointments each year. And pregnancy is only one potentially devastating consequence of premarital sex. Sexually active teens are also at risk for sexually transmitted diseases, not to mention emotional and spiritual damage that can hinder future relationships.

Talk to your preteens and teens and keep talking to them. I don't mean lecturing and haranguing. Simply keep the lines of communication open. Make it clear where you stand and why, but also that you will love them no matter what and help them in any way you can. (If you are a single mom, what you model will go a long way in influencing your children.) Most important, don't give up!

Here's an idea from family advocates James and Shirley Dobson that you might consider trying:

Years ago, when our daughter, Danae, was a preteen, we presented her with a small gold key. It was attached to a chain worn around her neck and represented the key to her heart. She made a vow then to give that key to one man only—the one who would share her love through the remainder of her life. In a similar way, you could present a special ring to your son. These symbols provide tangible reminders of the lasting, precious gifts of abstinence until marriage.[8]

SHOWING LOVE

One of the greatest struggles in our hurry-up, do-more, worn-out world is finding time to spend with our children. And yet time is what often communicates love more than anything else. Gifts and toys and clothes don't rank nearly as high on the love scale as an afternoon at the zoo, an evening alongside your child enjoying his or her favorite hobby, or even a morning spent doing chores *together*.

Even while weary parents struggle to find more time to spend with their children, one sure way to show children that they are cherished is something I like to call heart language —listening and speaking in love.

Listening—really listening—is one of the most valuable gifts we can give. In fact, some psychologists say that in the minds of children, listening is closely related to love.

But being a good listener isn't always easy—and it certainly isn't easy for me. I tend to be too quick to jump in with advice before I've heard the whole problem, too quick to give my viewpoint before I've been attentive to another person's idea. Sometimes I think God wrote the verse in James 1:19 just for me: "My dear brothers and sisters, be quick to listen, *s-l-o-w* to speak."[9]

Listening without interruption may not come naturally to everyone, but I've found that it is a skill anyone can learn—and well worth it. One practice I try to remember is to intentionally restrict my initial responses to expressions like "Hmmm," "Uh-huh," and "What else?" I've also learned the importance of making myself available when kids (husband, friends, or coworkers) *want* to talk. To say, "Let's get together later" often means not getting together at all.

When our youngest son was a teenager, he often felt like talking just as I was ready to fall into bed. We would pass in the hallways about eleven at night, and James would ask, "Hey, Mom, got a minute?" So we'd sit in the hallway, our backs resting against the wall. There was something about the late hour and the dim light that made his talking and my listening easier. Looking back, those were some of the best talks we ever had together.

As much as teens need moms to listen, so do toddlers. Have you ever thought what it is like for a toddler to follow adults around and try to get them to listen? All a little one sees is legs! When Al and I taught the preschool children at church, we learned how important it is to get down to their eye level. I remember one child saying, "Teacher, I like it when you get down here. It makes me feel good." Face-to-face listening with undivided attention seems to satisfy little hearts (and big ones, too).

Listening to children with love makes such a difference. But what you say is important, too. That's the other side of

Listening is the secret passage into the heart of a child.

KIMBER ANNIE ENGSTROM

heart language—speaking with love. Children as well as adults thrive on words of uplift and encouragement, and even words of discipline can be softened by gentleness and love. Remember the idea of "7=1" I mentioned in chapter 3?

Children thrive when your words and your tone tell them they are loved and valued.

In *Leaving the Light On,* John Trent tells a beautiful story about a little girl who is feeling out of sorts. One Saturday morning, the dad tells his little girl that he wants to take her on a date at her favorite restaurant—she can choose. Within an hour, they're sliding into a booth at McDonald's. Before they start in on their foam platters of eggs and pancakes, the dad takes his little girl's hand and tells her how thankful he is that she belongs to their family. He uses words like *treasure* and *precious*, and he points out some specific things about her that he loves.

When the father finally picks up his fork to start eating, the little girl pushes his hand back down and softly pleads, "Longer, Daddy . . . longer." So once again he takes her hand and tells her how much she means to him. Three more times he hears, "Longer, Daddy . . . longer" and complies. Then, when they finally get home, he hears her skip into the kitchen and announce to her mom, "Guess what! I'm special. Daddy told me so."[10]

Children long to feel they're special because someone told them so. You can be that person.

So Much More

There is so much more to say about the role of a godly mother —helping your children discover and develop their strengths, showing unconditional love, giving forgiveness, persevering in the tough times, disciplining appropriately, helping dreams come true—the list goes on and on. And no matter how many words are written, they only begin to touch the absolute wonder—and awesome responsibility—of motherhood. Always remember that nothing you ever do will matter as much as pouring your life into the precious souls God has entrusted to you.

Too quickly, the backyard swing is still, the prom pictures are put away, and the bedrooms are empty. As you look back, you might wonder if you really made a difference.

Yes, dear one, you did. And you still can. Even after children are grown—and even if they haven't followed the path of faith you modeled—you still have a powerful influence.

So don't give up. Keep praying. Keep hoping.

Your children will never forget their heartprints of home.

The Mailbox

The following story by Patty Duncan is a sweet reminder that sometimes it's the little things than make a child feel cherished.

"You're a wonderful Mother," I wrote on the Mother's Day card with the picture of sunflowers, garden gloves, and a watering can. "You were always home for me after school, with warm cookies and milk. You led our 4-H club and worked in PTA. Best of all, now you're my friend."

I walked out the gravel driveway to the mailbox, opened the metal door, and slid in the card. As I shut the door and pulled up the red flag, I remembered another mailbox from long ago.

As a child I spent hours in a small playhouse in the back yard. I decked it out with curtains strung on twine, a window box planted with marigolds, and a mailbox made from a coffee can.

The can was nailed to the outside wall of the playhouse, next to the window. It was painted with green house paint and fitted with a small board inside to create a flat horizontal surface.

One languid summer day I ran into the house and found my mother mopping the kitchen floor. "Mama," I asked, "could you bring me some mail?"

She straightened up and held the mop in one hand, massaging the small of her back with the other. She looked down at me and smiled. Her bright blue eyes softened as she looked at me, her suntanned, pigtailed daughter.

"Well, yes, I think I can, after I finish the floor," she said. "You go back to the playhouse and wait awhile. I'll be there."

So I ran outside, letting the screen door slam behind me. I skipped down the narrow brick path to the clothesline and under it to the playhouse beside the dwarf apple tree. I busied myself with little-girl housekeeping: washing my doll dishes, tidying the bed, sweeping the floor with the toy corn straw broom.

Then I heard steps on the brick path. "Mail time," Mama called in a high voice. Then I heard the thunk of envelopes firmly striking the inside of the coffee can.

I waited to give her time to walk back to the house, then rushed out of the playhouse and reached into the can to grab my treasure. Shuffling through it, I found three envelopes, a catalog, and a small package. What a haul!

I sat on the grass that sloped down to the garden to open it. Naturally, I went for the package first. Tearing away the brown grocery sack paper, I lifted the lid from a tiny box. Wow! Two sticks of Juicy Fruit gum; a square of waxed paper wrapped around a handful of chocolate chips, raisins, and miniature marshmallows; and a new Pink Pearl eraser. I munched on the snack mixture while I explored the rest of my mail.

Thumbing through the seed catalog, I enjoyed the brightly-colored flower pictures. Then I spread the envelopes out in my hand. Each was addressed to "Patty, Playhouse, Back Yard, Oregon" and posted with an S & H Green Stamp. I slipped my finger under the flap of one and ripped it open. It held a flyer from a car insurance company. In the next I found an advertisement for magazine subscriptions with a hundred tiny stamps to stick onto the order form. From the last envelope I pulled a page of note paper.

"How are you doing?" I read in my mother's perfect printing. "It's been beautiful weather here, though a little hot for me. I've been canning beans. We have a lovely, large garden, as usual. Do come visit us. You know you are always welcome. Love, Mama."

She signed it in "writing" with swirls at the beginning of the "M" and at the end of the "a."

That was 40 years ago.

I thought Mama and I had become close friends only recently. But remembering the mailbox, I realized I was wrong. The mother who took the time from her mopping and canning to gather up some junk mail and trinkets to put into a package, write a personal note, and deliver it all in true play-acting style was my special companion even back then.

She was always my friend.

PATTY DUNCAN
From *Christian Women Today*[11]

A GENTLE TOUCH
For discussion or journaling

*I have no greater joy than to hear
that my children are walking in the truth.*

3 JOHN 1:4[12]

1. What are some of your favorite memories from your childhood days? How have they shaped you?

2. In what ways do you think you have been successful in nurturing faith, teaching character, and showing love to your children?

3. If someone with children younger than yours asked you for advice on how to nurture children in the Christian faith and moral values, how would you encourage her?

4. Write a paragraph or two in honor of your mother. If she is still alive, consider giving it to her as a gift. If not, share what you have written with your family or a friend. (If memories of home are sad for you, write a letter to someone else who had a positive influence on your life. Or consider writing a note of forgiveness for the heartbreaks of your home life.)

A Prayer from the Heart

Dear Lord,

It seems that just yesterday the children were newborns, and now they are growing so big. Please help me watch over them and guide them and encourage them. When they fall, help me to lift them up and guide them back to the path that leads to You. And most of all, Lord, thank You for loving my children even more than I do. ♡

CHAPTER 7

The Beauty of Time

*Some people, no matter how old they get,
never lose their beauty—
they merely move it from their faces
into their hearts.*

MARTIN BUXBAUM

*D*uring the past few days, I've been thinking about the older women who have had a significant influence in my life. Sometimes with tears sliding down my cheeks and sometimes with little chuckles that rolled out into full laughter, I've pulled the memories from my heart.

A few of these women are in heaven now. Most are in the autumn or winter of their lives—but I certainly don't consider them to be over the hill. Instead, they are the kind of women who shield their eyes from the sun and look into the distance for more hills to climb. Their faces may show the accumulation of years, but there is a radiance about them that far surpasses any "botoxed" smile.

They look at life as something to be celebrated, and commemorate milestone birthdays as lifelines instead of deadlines. If you could work alongside them in your office, meet them for coffee, or study the Bible under their mentorship, you would quickly discover the incredible beauty of their years.

Do you, too, know a woman like that?

Just as important, are you on your way toward becoming one?

GODLY OLDER WOMEN

Over the years, my most influential "older women" have been dear family members—my own mother, Al's mother, my sister.

But there are many others who have, and still do, make a difference in my daily walk with Christ. Like their counterparts described in Titus 2:3, these are women more mature in the Lord than I who have been willing to open their hearts, take my hand, and let me learn from their ways.

What a lovely fabric they weave in my memory. Widowed, single, married for more than fifty years, divorced by an unfaithful husband. Childless, grandmothers, entrepreneurs, mothers-at-home, very rich, of humble means, knowing years of happiness, knowing years of heartbreak. And through the lovely design there is a golden thread that makes the pattern all the more beautiful. These are godly women—every one. And the habits I learned from them are the very habits I try to model to younger women. Their stories are part of my story. What they have lived, I try to live, too.

It seems I'm a lot like the little boy in chapter 6 who walked behind his mother in order to follow in Jesus' footsteps. I'm trying to follow in the footsteps of women who walk a lot like Jesus.

Footsteps to Follow

Some people are intimidated when they read about the worthy woman described in Proverbs 31:10–31. They feel she is an unattainable role model for the twenty-first century. In some ways I can understand their frustration, but I love reading these verses anyway. Perhaps the difference for me is that instead of feeling intimidated about what the Proverbs 31 woman *does*, I feel inspired by who she *is*. When I consider her character, her virtue, her industriousness, her compassion, and her faithfulness—it seems to me that hers are ideal footsteps to follow.

Since many attributes of the Proverbs 31 woman are covered elsewhere in this book, for this chapter I just want to mention three qualities found in verses 25 and 26—qualities that the godly older women in my life all have in common:

> She is clothed with strength and dignity,
> and she laughs with no fear of the future.
> When she speaks, her words are wise.[1]

Clothed with Strength and Dignity

Of the older women I admire, all have strength and dignity. By that I don't mean they are domineering or bossy, but they are persuasively strong in standing up for what they believe. These faithful women seem to have no problem embracing the never-changing truth of God's Word in an ever-changing culture. People who have different standards aren't put off by their high morals. Instead, because they are so gracious in their actions, these godly women are like giant magnets pulling people into the circle of God's love.

They are strong concerning their physical well-being, too. They accept the limitations that come with aging, but never use getting older as a reason to avoid physical fitness. They join Curves, pump iron, and walk daily miles in the same kinds of weather as the postal carriers (neither rain, nor hail, nor sleet . . .). And quite remarkably, sometimes they eat more fiber than chocolate. They are definitely amazing women!

But one of the strengths I admire most is their determination to keep growing mentally and to keep pursuing their dreams. Returning to college, taking up oil painting, starting businesses, using computers, learning to ride a Harley, going on short mission trips, volunteering at hospitals—the list is long and impressive. Even those whose activities are somewhat curtailed find ways to be active and useful and enjoy whatever life has to offer.

> *Life should not be a journey to the grave with the intention of arriving safely in a pretty and well-preserved body, but rather to skid in broadside, thoroughly used up, totally worn out, and loudly proclaiming, "Wow! What a ride!"*
>
> AUTHOR UNKNOWN

One of my favorite authors, Howard Hendricks, tells a story that wonderfully exemplifies an older woman with strength and dignity. The story is about one of his best friends, a woman who was quite a bit his senior. One day when she was eighty-six, they both showed up at a rather boring dinner party. She walked up to him and said, "Well, Hendricks, I haven't seen you for a long time. What are the five best books you've read in the past year?"

This was the same woman who, at age eighty-three, went on a tour of the Holy Land with a group of NFL football players. One of Hendricks's most vivid memories of that trip is seeing her out in front and yelling back to them, "Come on, men, get with it!"

And a week before she died in her sleep at her daughter's home, this same woman sat down and wrote out her goals for the next ten years.

As Howard Hendricks says, "May her tribe increase!"

She Laughs with No Fear of the Future

No wonder my friends keep sending me e-mail jokes about aging! They've read that the awesome Proverbs 31 woman laughs with no fear of the future. And they are great advocates of Proverbs 17:22: "A merry heart does good, like medicine." In fact, here's an e-mail one of them forwarded this week:

> Great news: laughing heartily one hundred times is the phys-
> iological equivalent to working out on a rowing machine for
> ten minutes. The problem is, once I get going, I'm afraid I
> won't be able to stop and I'll laugh myself into anorexia!

As wonderful as humor is, laughing with no fear of the future means something much deeper. It's about having a sacred and unshakable trust in God. It's knowing that God is our refuge in the severest storms. It's believing that nothing can separate us from the love of God that is in Christ Jesus. It's being confident that when the last valley must be crossed, the Good Shepherd will still be walking with us.[2]

When I consider the older women who make a difference in my life, they have this kind of trust. Instead of trying to fig-ure out all of life's unanswerables, they resolutely cling to their faith in God when tough times come. Even during the deepest disappointments and darkest storms, they are not afraid, because they know God holds their future in His hands.

Their unquestioning trust in God reminds me of a sweet story I heard years ago. It was about a ship that set sail from New York to Liverpool with the captain's daughter on board. One night a sudden and terrible storm arose. The waves crashed over the deck, and the winds were so strong, they almost capsized the vessel. Passengers scrambled from their berths in fear for their lives. The captain's young daughter, only eight years old, awoke to the confusion and cried out, asking what was happening. They told her of the storm, and she asked, "Is Father at the helm?" When they assured her that he was, she pulled the covers up to her chin, snuggled into the pillow, and in spite of the crashing waves, fell back to sleep.

Life may not be the party we hoped for. But while we are here, we might as well dance.

FROM AN EIGHTY-THREE-YEAR-OLD WOMAN

Facing the storms of life without fear is just one of the lessons I've learned from godly older women. When dark waves came crashing over their happiness, I've seen them cry and grieve and cry some more, but it was easy to understand that these were tears of sorrow, not of fear.

My own mother, now gone to be with the Lord, was this kind of woman. Because she had known so many heartbreaks in her life, she was especially good at comforting others. Being careful to make sure that the timing was just right, my mother would sometimes share the words of Ecclesiastes: "To everything there is a season . . . a time to weep, and a time to laugh; a time to mourn, and a time to dance."[3] Holding another dear woman's hands in her own, my mother would whisper, "Now is the time to weep, but God will bring a time to dance again."

And the time to dance did come. Little by little, as my mother predicted, their broken hearts did mend. And little by little, taught by her example, they learned (and I am learning, too) to laugh with no fear of the future.

WHEN SHE SPEAKS, HER WORDS ARE WISE

A few weeks ago, someone asked me how I had become so wise. That was a shock—I don't think of myself as wise at all. (I used to think that when I was in my twenties, but not now!) Nevertheless, I answered, "Oh, it's probably just because I've lived a long time."

Age is certainly part of the secret to wisdom, I suppose. But the more important part of becoming wise is learning the precepts of God's Word.

I like seeking counsel from godly older women. I like it because they don't jump in right away and give quick answers as though the solutions are obvious. They listen for a long time without interrupting and then ask questions, such as, "What have you tried so far?" "What works and what doesn't?" "What do you think God wants you to do?" (That's an especially good one!) All the while they are listening, I can almost see their minds scanning the Scriptures for just the right kind of counsel.

Then, when they finally give advice, their words are like gentle rain falling on dry places. Their counsel is like that described in James 3:17: "The wisdom that is from above is first pure, then peaceable, gentle, willing to yield, full of mercy and good fruits, without partiality and without hypocrisy."

I especially love it when godly women sit next to me and open their Bibles to show me passages that relate to my problems. The pages are worn, verses are underlined, hearts and notes fill the margins. It's obvious they are *very* familiar with God's Love Letter, which is also His Handbook of Wisdom. Some of these women make it their daily habit to read selected passages recommended in a daily devotional book. Many make use of a variety of study aids. And quite a few have a habit of reading the Bible all the way through each year.

> *If you don't have a Bible, get one.*
> *If you've got a Bible, read it.*
> *If you read the Bible, believe it.*
> *If you believe the Bible, live it.*
>
> FROM *LIFE'S LITTLE HANDBOOK OF WISDOM*

I discovered that one dear woman I know reads a new Bible through every year, making notes and markings as she reads. Then, at the end of the year, she gives the Bible to someone dear to her.

My, what a treasured gift that would be—a treasury of wisdom.

THE MEASURE OF BEAUTY

Lying open on my desk is a recent issue of *AARP* magazine, the leading periodical for people over fifty. The headline reads "Hollywood's Hottest," right above a photo of seven fabulous women.[5] The youngest in this group of alluring women is only forty-five, three are in their late fifties, and the others—unbelievably—are past seventy. The inside article quotes French fashion designer Coco Chanel as saying, "You can be gorgeous at twenty, charming at forty, and irresistible for the rest of your life."

Thank you Ms. Chanel. I like the idea of being irresistible, but the truth is no amount of makeup, sparkling diamonds, or glamorous gowns will make me sizzle like these Oscar-winning cover girls. I'm not even sure an extreme makeover would help much. In fact, I'm so discouraged that I'll just go to the kitchen and fix myself a nice hot-fudge sundae. (Just kidding!)

I have to admit that these Hollywood beauties are fascinating to look at and that some of them have come through tough times with admirable accomplishments to their credit. But after writing this chapter about the godly influence of older Christian women, I find that these cover girls hardly shine at all. And this isn't sour grapes about the glamour of movie stars; it's just that the beauty in the older women who have inspired me seems far more irresistible than the beauty of Hollywood.

Theirs is the beauty described in 1 Peter 3:3–4: "Do not let your adornment be merely outward—arranging the hair, wearing gold, or putting on fine apparel—rather let it be the hidden person of the heart, with the incorruptible beauty of a gentle and quiet spirit, which is very precious in the sight of God."

It's the kind of beauty I want for myself, and for you as well, which brings me to the close of this chapter and the two hopes I have for you.

First, I hope you will recognize your potential to become a beautiful "older woman" for someone else. You don't have to wait until you're old enough for AARP! If you are twenty, you can speak wisdom to a teenage girl. If you are thirty, you have a wealth of experience to offer to someone in her twenties. An empty-nester has much to offer the mother of preschoolers; a retiree can counsel a woman approaching menopause. And so on and so on. No matter how much "older" you are, you can help another woman be stronger, more fearless, more faithful. Your time, your teaching, and your example can be tangible acts of grace in their lives.

My second hope for you is that you, too, will find godly older women to influence your life like those I have known.

You won't have to search very hard. They are everywhere. Just look for the women who have wrinkled faces and unwrinkled hearts.

Verna's Secret

As you will discover in this inspiring story by Linda Andersen, sometimes we make the wrong assumptions about older women. Once we really get to know them, often the serenity of their simple lifestyle is what changes our lives the most.

She lives alone in tiny, second-story rooms above a weather-beaten general store and gas station that have seen better days. No one has used them for years. Verna Bok has been a widow for 40 years, I learned one Sunday after church. This diminutive lady without a car is always in church (when she's well), and she's always smiling. I wondered why as I watched her come and go, leaning heavily on her cane.

The blinds at Verna's windows are slightly askew and the building she lives in looks perpetually deserted and forgotten. A lone gas pump sits stolidly out in front near the road like a paunchy, middle-aged man with nothing much to do except watch the traffic go by. The old, sun-faded pump hasn't served our lazy little community in more years than anyone can remember. The cost of gasoline still reads 31 cents a gallon—just as if inflation never happened—just as if it remembers a time when our tiny farming town boasted enough "live" businesses to keep the main road buzzing with activity. Verna remembers those days well enough. Now business has gone elsewhere, leaving the village of Forest Grove and Verna to grow old together. But Verna Bok is not a person who merely sits still and grows old, as I soon discovered.

I was having some neighbors in one evening, and on a sudden impulse I decided to include Verna.

"How nice!" she beamed over the telephone wire connecting our voices. "How very nice of you to call. I'd surely come if I was well enough." She had been sick for a couple of weeks up there alone in that tiny apartment. I was sorry, and I told her so.

"You must get awfully lonesome, Verna."

"Lonesome?" She sounded surprised. "Oh my, no," she bubbled, laughing. "Why, I'm never lonesome." (I had a feeling I was about to discover something.) "You see, I have all my good memories to keep me company—and my photograph albums too. And then, 'a course, I keep so busy with Ruth's boys."

"Oh?" I asked, before remembering that she had a nearby neighbor named Ruth.

"Oh yes," she replied. "You see, Ruth has raised them eight boys by herself ever since the divorce, and she works, ya know. So's I fix supper for them boys every night. Yes, I been doin' it for years. It saves her a whole lot of worry and it gives me sumthin' useful to do. Oh, yes, them boys gets me flowers too, on Mother's Day. They're like m'own boys." Now I knew that this was an unusual person indeed. And I began to understand the secret of her youthful exuberance for life.

Verna had learned something that most people take a lifetime to discover, and she had found it less than a country mile from her own home. Without actually looking for happiness, she had kept herself busy filling the empty cups of other people's lives.

When my husband greeted Verna in church one morning some weeks later, he commented on the stunning pair of cardinals he had spotted in our maple trees. "Verna," he emphasized, "they would have knocked your eyes out!" Her warm eyes brightened, and her familiar smile appeared.

"Oh yes," she chuckled. "And you know, I heard the most beautiful wren song just this morning." She shook her finger for emphasis as she talked. "I get up early every day, ya know, so's I don't miss a thing. I like to watch the houses around here wake up, don'tcha know. Yessir, there's so much ta see— so much ta see. And I enjoy everything God has made— everything, don'tcha see?" The secret was finally out.

Verna, you get up to see what most of us miss, or ignore, or are just too busy to enjoy. You magnify the plusses God places all over your small world. You seem to paint a rainbow around every little event, even the early morning song of a little bird. There's no need to feel sorry for you, Verna. None whatever. You have no time to feel sorry for yourself. You're too busy giving thanks and enjoying things.

Keep it up, Verna. Your sunshiny ways are bringing God's light to a lot of lives—including mine.

LINDA ANDERSEN
from *Slices of Life*[6]

A GENTLE TOUCH
For journaling or discussion

O God, You have taught me from my youth;
And to this day I declare Your wondrous works.
Now also when I am old and grayheaded,
O God, do not forsake me,
Until I declare Your strength to this generation,
Your power to everyone who is to come.

PSALM 71:17–18

1. Describe an older woman who has been a godly influence in your life.

2. The Quakers call the years of growing older "the season of soul making." What do you think they mean?

3. What kind of woman do you want to be ten years from now?

A Prayer from the Heart

Dear Lord,

I often forget how old I am growing, and I'm almost startled when I look into the mirror and see the accumulation of years. I gently pull up my cheeks to see how my face would look with fewer wrinkles—sighing when I let them relax again. Thank You for the example and inspiration of godly older women in my life—and thank You for the opportunity to be an instrument of Your grace in a younger woman's life. Is it really possible that someone else might see a godly beauty in my years? And, more important, Lord, do You see Your beauty in me? ♡

CHAPTER 8

Even the Least

When Christ said, "I was hungry and you fed me,"
He didn't mean only the hunger for bread and food;
He also meant the hunger to be loved.

MOTHER TERESA

When I was in school, I always dreaded walking into a classroom on Monday mornings and hearing the teacher announce, "Okay, everyone get out your pencils. We're having a pop quiz today." Groan. Teachers who gave pop quizzes were never my favorites. My favorite teachers were the ones who let you know beforehand that a test was coming up, the ones who would give hints on how to prepare and explain how the test would affect the final grade. I always did better when I knew what to expect.

In the last sermon recorded by Matthew, Jesus told his followers about a test that will take place when He returns. He wasn't telling a parable. He was sharing the details of an actual event that is still in the future. And it won't be a pop quiz because He let us know in advance how important it is and how we can get ready for it.

> When God measures
> a person,
> He puts the tape around
> the heart,
> not around the head.
>
> AUTHOR UNKNOWN

It will be a test that measures the character of our heart—and our love of Jesus Christ.

As Jesus told it, everyone will be there—Jesus, the angels, all the nations, you and I—everyone. He will begin by dividing the people into two groups—"sheep" and "goats," good and evil, those who are to be at His right and those to be at His left.

How will He choose which group each person goes in? Listen to how Jesus answers that question when He describes the scene in Matthew 25:34–46:

> Then the King will say to those on the right, "Come, you who are blessed by my Father, inherit the Kingdom prepared for you from the foundation of the world. For I was hungry, and you fed me. I was thirsty, and you gave me a drink. I was a stranger, and you invited me into your home. I was naked, and you gave me clothing. I was sick, and you cared for me. I was in prison, and you visited me. . . . I assure you, when you did it to one of the least of these my brothers and sisters, you were doing it to me!"
>
> Then the King will turn to those on the left and say, "Away with you, you cursed ones, into the eternal fire prepared for the Devil and his demons! For I was hungry, and you didn't feed me. I was thirsty, and you didn't give me anything to drink. I was a stranger, and you didn't invite me into your home. I was naked, and you gave me no clothing. I was sick and in prison, and you didn't visit me. . . . I assure you, when you refused to help the least of these my brothers and sisters, you were refusing to help me." And they will go away into eternal punishment, but the righteous will go into eternal life.[1]

I wonder if I will ever understand the depth of meaning in this passage. Will I ever fully grasp that the many times I have ignored those in need, I have actually ignored Jesus?

I've passed Him by without notice or compassion, my heart remaining unbroken and untouched.

And yet, there have been a few precious times where I *have* cared for "the least" of God's children . . . and those are the sweet moments when I have cared for Jesus Himself.

WHO ARE THE LEAST?

The first time I was asked to speak on this passage of Scripture, I sent dozens of notes to friends, family, coworkers, and people at church quoting the above passage from Matthew 25 and asking them how they would define "the least." Their replies included people who are lonely, homeless, hungry, trapped, misunderstood, diseased, broken, expendable, poor, unborn, insignificant, abused, abandoned, unsupported, afraid, neglected, overlooked, helpless, hopeless, unloved, and forgotten. Their comments were so thoughtful and kind that it seemed like they wanted to bathe the wounds of "the least" with tender words of compassion.

When speaking at church events, I often mention the answers I received and ask the women to share with me how they are reaching out to those who are helpless, hopeless, unloved, and forgotten. The answers are wonderful! In one community, a group of churches got together and organized a ministry called Room at the Inn. During the cold winter months, they take turns opening their churches to provide meals, beds, hot showers, sack lunches, and good conversation for homeless families.

In another town, a group of Christian beauticians get together once a month and give free haircuts and pedicures for women staying at a shelter for victims of domestic violence.

In a city across the country from me, a Bible study group from a local church went to the Salvation Army's shelter for women and decorated the dining hall with streamers in spring colors and beautiful centerpieces. That evening they served a catered meal and gave a gift to each woman and a stuffed animal to each child. The special speaker for the event was a woman from their church who had been raped and had previously struggled with substance abuse. She used her artistic talents on the potter's wheel to demonstrate how God can use even the most tragic circumstances to reshape our lives into beautiful vessels.

Many churches have food and clothing closets or serve meals to the hungry on a weekly basis. Men and women regularly pack up their Bibles and guitars to visit prisoners and lead Bible studies and sing familiar gospel hymns. Others faithfully give up their Sunday afternoons to provide worship services at nursing homes. High school kids donate their summer months to present fantastic vacation Bible schools for kids in the poorest parts of the inner city.

Several years ago, Rose and Frank Averill and their two teenagers volunteered at a summer camp in Florida for homeless children. After noticing how many of the kids didn't have shoes, they started using their own money to buy new shoes at discount stores and to distribute them to the needy. Soon neighbors, strangers, and local businesses heard about what they were doing and wanted to get involved. The project snowballed into Footprints Ministry, which now distributes hundreds of new shoes each month. As Rose Averill tells their volunteers, "We're giving the children and their parents more than shoes. We're distributing love and dignity."[2]

I'm forever amazed at the variety of stories about how churches and individuals are touching the lives of those we call "the least." And they love doing it! Their joy is effervescent, bubbling over, when they offer the gentle compassion of Christ to those with broken lives. And I can just imagine how they'll feel when Jesus opens His arms to them and says, "This way. Come over here and stand next to Me on the right."

A HEART OF COMPASSION

It seems that for as long as I have known her, my friend Marilyn has had a tender heart toward people who are broken. Tears come easily to her as she prays for the homeless men and women living in tents or cardboard shacks under the bridges in Portland, Oregon. But Marilyn's involvement with these street people goes deeper than tears.

Week after week for several years, my friend drove to the drop-in center at the Salvation Army to serve coffee to the street people. Yes, she was the one I mentioned in chapter 3, the one who reached out to touch a woman named Margaret. And over time, Margaret and a dozen others became Marilyn's special friends. Listening to their stories, buying shoes, eating meals together, helping them get set up in apartments, and introducing them to her own friends and family were all part of the love she felt for them. It wasn't about fixing their lives, although she certainly hoped and prayed that their lives would improve. Very simply, she wanted to go where people hurt and to love them for Jesus Christ.

How do we develop that kind of compassion? I believe the first step is to ask God to make our hearts tender so we *really* see those who are in pain, those who are lonely, fearful, and helpless. In Marilyn's case, her soul was stirred when she watched a television report about the terrible plight of the homeless during the winter months. She didn't switch the program off. Instead, she listened intently, opened her heart to their suffering, and sought out ways she could help.

> *The difference between the person on the street and the one who drives by in the backseat of a limo can be a few short missteps, a thin line of privilege, or a blown opportunity. Life is fragile, as are the means by which we position ourselves in society.*
>
> JOHN FISCHER

I heard a story about a man whose response to an obvious need was just the opposite of Marilyn's response. It happened not too far from where I worked at the time. A Christian businessman was driving to lunch with two of his associates. When they were a few blocks from the restaurant, he saw a man passed out by the curb. They were on East Burnside, in an older part of town that hosts some longtime business establishments as well as street people. Because the man on the curb was disheveled, it was easy to assume he was a wino passed out from too much alcohol. Even so, it bothered the businessman that when people crossed the street they just stepped around the fallen man as though he were invisible. He commented to his two associates that he couldn't believe no one was stopping to help.

On the way back from lunch, the man drove by the same corner. "Look, he's still there. Can you believe it?" Then the signal changed, and the Christian businessman and his two friends drove through the intersection and on to the office without another thought about the disheveled man passed out by the curb.

Doesn't it make you angry to hear that? And doesn't your heart weep? Me, too. But then I must stop and ask myself how many times I have walked or driven by as if those in need were invisible.

After hearing this story, my husband and I walked the streets of that same neighborhood. We asked the Lord to break our hearts for the people who were so poor and sad. We tried to interact with them, to smile, to encourage, to touch a shoulder, to share a sandwich. But we were strangers. We were those who *have*—families, friends, a home, a car, a job, warm clothes, money—walking among those who *have not*. They diverted their eyes and would not look into our faces even when they asked for coins. We gladly gave them what they asked, though some had told us not to. And all the way home we wept together, realizing it takes a greater involvement than an occasional walk down East Burnside to make a difference in the world of the least of these.

REACHING OUT

If the first step in developing a heart of compassion is asking God to help us *really* see those who are hurting, then the second step is reaching out, doing what we can to respond to the need we see. How did Al and I do that? Well, after our day of walking the streets of East Burnside, we found we were more generous in giving money to organizations that feed the hungry or house the homeless or minister to prisoners. But the biggest change in us was our attitude toward individuals who stood on corners with cardboard signs asking for food or help. We no longer had thoughts like, *Well, if they really need money, they could get a job.* And we no longer could look the other way and drive by.

For a while we made up sack meals with juice, granola bars, beef jerky, and crackers and cheese packs—items that would keep without refrigeration. We carried them in our car and handed the sacks out the window. After a few months, we decided that whenever possible (unless we were running late for a wedding or something urgent like that), we would drive to the nearest fast-food place, get the biggest meal, and take it to the person on the corner. We'd get out of the car, offer the meal in Jesus' name, and visit for a few moments. More than once, people asked if we would pray for them. And we did— right there on the street corner, holding hands.

Oh, I know, these are small efforts. Certainly there are other people who do much more. But they are beginning steps that anyone can do. Besides, as we have continued to respond this way to the needs we see, our hearts have grown more and more tender toward weary, hurting people. And I truly believe this is what Jesus wants for us as we try to follow His heart. He wants us to *see* the hungry and the thirsty and the naked and the prisoners . . . and to love them the way He does.

Mother Teresa of Calcutta once had a conversation with a famous model about reaching out to others. "I know," the beautiful young woman said, "you want me to write out a big check and give my money away."

Mother Teresa's response to the model is probably the best advice any of us could receive.

"Oh, no," she answered. "I want you to do something much harder. I want you to find someone lonely and forgotten and give your love away."

MAKING A DIFFERENCE

If you are like me, sometimes you might feel discouraged or at least overwhelmed because there are so many needy people, so many hungry souls. You wonder if anything you do can really make a difference in a world filled with hurt. When I feel that way, I like to think of the following often-told story.

There was an old man who lived along the Atlantic coastline, and each morning when the tide went out, he walked for miles along the beach. Every so often, he would stoop down, gently lift something from the sand, and then toss it into the ocean. He repeated this strange behavior every single day.

One morning a curious neighbor followed him to try and

figure out what he was doing. It didn't take long to see that the man was picking up starfish that had been stranded by the retreating tide and throwing them back into the ocean so they wouldn't die of dehydration in the hot summer sun.

The neighbor chuckled to himself and then called out in a sarcastic tone, "Hey, old man. This beach runs for hundreds of miles, and there are thousands of starfish stranded on the sand every day. Do you really think that throwing a few back is making a difference?"

The old man turned toward his neighbor and then looked down at the one starfish he held in his hand. A smile spread across his face as he answered, "Well, it makes a difference to this one."

And so it is with us when we reach out to someone. We can make a difference in that one person's life. And then another's and another's and another's. We can change our world one dear person at a time.

The Tattooed Stranger

*Although I've never met Susan Fahncke in person, I've used
several of her short stories in the Stories for the Heart book
collection. To me, her words are always like a sweet fragrance coming from a summer garden. I know "The Tattooed
Stranger" will tug on your heart just as it tugged on mine.*

He was kind of scary. He sat there on the grass with his
cardboard sign, his dog (actually his dog was adorable), and
tattoos running up and down both arms and even on his
neck. His sign proclaimed him to be "stuck and hungry" and
to please help.

I'm a sucker for anyone needing help. My husband both
hates and loves this quality in me.

I pulled the van over and in my rearview mirror, contem-
plated this man, tattoos and all. He was youngish, maybe
forty. He wore one of those bandannas tied over his head,
biker/pirate style. Anyone could see he was dirty and had a
scraggly beard. But if you looked closer, you could see that
he had neatly tucked in the black T-shirt, and his things were
in a small, tidy bundle. Nobody was stopping for him. I
could see the other drivers take one look and immediately
focus on something else—anything else.

It was so hot out. I could see in the man's very blue eyes how dejected and tired and worn-out he felt. The sweat was trickling down his face. As I sat with the air-conditioning blowing, the Scripture suddenly popped into my head. "Inasmuch as ye have done it unto the least of these, my brethren, so ye have done it unto me."

I reached down into my purse and extracted a ten-dollar bill. My twelve-year-old son, Nick, knew right away what I was doing. "Can I take it to him, Mom?"

"Be careful, honey," I warned and handed him the money. I watched in the mirror as he rushed over to the man, and with a shy smile, handed it to him. I saw the man, startled, stand and take the money, putting it into his back pocket. "Good," I thought to myself, "now he will at least have a hot meal tonight." I felt satisfied, proud of myself. I had made a sacrifice and now I could go on with my errands.

When Nick got back into the car, he looked at me with sad, pleading eyes. "Mom, his dog looks so hot and the man is really nice." I knew I had to do more.

"Go back and tell him to stay there, that we will be back in fifteen minutes," I told Nick. He bounded out of the car and ran to tell the tattooed stranger.

We then ran to the nearest store and bought our gifts carefully. "It can't be too heavy," I explained to the children. "He has to be able to carry it around with him." We finally settled on our purchases. A bag of "Ol' Roy" (I hoped it was good— it looked good enough for me to eat! How do they make dog food look that way?); a flavored chew-toy shaped like a bone; a water dish; bacon-flavored snacks (for the dog); two bottles of water (one for the dog, one for Mr. Tattoos); and some people snacks for the man.

We rushed back to the spot where we had left him, and there he was, still waiting. And still nobody else was stopping for him. With hands shaking, I grabbed our bags and climbed out of the car, all four of my children following me, each carrying gifts. As we walked up to him, I had a fleeting moment of fear, hoping he wasn't a serial killer.

I looked into his eyes and saw something that startled me and made me ashamed of my judgment. I saw tears. He was fighting like a little boy to hold back his tears. How long had it been since someone showed this man kindness? I told him I hoped it wasn't too heavy for him to carry and showed him what we had brought. He stood there, like a child at Christmas, and I felt like my small contributions were so inadequate. When I took out the water dish, he snatched it out of my hands as if it were solid gold and told me he had no way to give his dog water. He gingerly set it down, filled it with the bottled water we brought, and stood up to look directly into my eyes. His were so blue, so intense, and my own filled with tears as he said, "Ma'am, I don't know what to say." He then put both hands on his bandanna-clad head and just started to cry. This man, this "scary" man, was so gentle, so sweet, so humble.

I smiled through my tears and said, "Don't say anything." Then I noticed the tattoo on his neck. It said, "Mama tried."

As we all piled into the van and drove away, he was on his knees, arms around his dog, kissing his nose and smiling. I waved cheerfully and then finally broke down in tears.

I have so much. My worries seem so trivial and petty now. I have a home, a loving husband, four beautiful children. I have a bed. I wondered where he would sleep tonight.

My stepdaughter, Brandie, turned to me and said in the sweetest little-girl voice, "I feel so good."

Although it seemed as if we had helped him, the man with the tattoos gave us a gift that I will never forget. He taught us that no matter what the outside looks like, inside each of us is a human being deserving of kindness, of compassion, of acceptance. He opened my heart.

Tonight and every night I will pray for the gentle man with the tattoos and his dog. And I will hope that God will send more people like him into my life to remind me what's really important.

SUSAN FAHNCKE
Quoted in *Stories for a Faithful Heart*[3]

A GENTLE TOUCH
For discussion or journaling

*But if anyone has enough money to live well
and sees a brother or sister in need and refuses
to help—how can God's love be in that person?*

1 JOHN 3:17[4]

1. What is your customary response when you see a homeless person begging on the sidewalk? What fears and reasonable questions typically keep you from responding? How do you think Jesus would speak to those fears?

2. Have you or a family member or close friend ever been in a desperate situation where it was necessary to depend on others for help? Or have you ever been the one who provided help to someone in desperate need? Describe your feelings about either needing help or being able to give help.

3. Glance back at the chapter. Is there something in it that tugs at your heart? If so, what can you do in the next five days so you won't ignore or forget about the tugging?

A Prayer from the Heart

Dear Lord,

I long to have a heart of compassion. Please help me understand how I can ease the hurt and loneliness of others. On that glorious day when I behold Your face, I want to feel Your pleasure—to hear You say that when I touched another's life, I touched Yours. ♡

CHAPTER 9

Lost and Found

If you meet me and you forget about me,
you have lost nothing of value.
If you meet Jesus Christ and forget about Him,
you have lost everything of value.

AUTHOR UNKNOWN

I couldn't ignore the poster. Even though I was rushing out the door, eager to get home, I had to stop and look.

It hung right by the main exit of the Christian bookstore. A quick glance was not enough. Although I wanted to turn away, I kept looking and somehow knew I would never forget it. Almost thirty years have passed, but I can still close my eyes and vividly recall the details. And, yes, the tears still come.

The poster was titled "The Church Potluck." It depicted a large, deep-looking lake. Whitecaps broke the surface, licking the sides of a dock where three long serving tables had been lined up. The tables were covered with white paper cloths and laden with macaroni casseroles, gelatin salads, apple pies, and chocolate brownies. The people standing around the tables were obviously having a good time—eating, conversing, laughing, hugging—and were not the least bit aware that all around them, in the lake, people were drowning.

My breath catches when I think about the possibility that we Christians can get so involved in enjoying one another's fellowship that we are oblivious to those who do not know Jesus Christ as Savior. There are drowning people in our neighborhoods, where we work and shop and exercise, where our kids play ball. They are headed toward a Christless eternity, an eternity of darkness instead of light, of sorrow instead of joy.

If we're not concerned about that reality, if we're not doing something about it, can we really be following God's heart?

GOOD NEWS

There was good news in the paper this morning. A young boy who had been lost in the wilderness for four days had been found. The newspaper photo showed him with his mother's arms wrapped around him, and the expression on their faces was pure joy.

It's a terrible thing to be lost—afraid of the darkness, wondering what will happen, and hoping with all your heart that someone will come looking for you. And *lost* is one of the terms the Bible uses for people who do not know Christ as Savior. They are like the drowning people in the poster or the little boy in the wilderness—desperately in need of help. And when they are rescued, their response is always the same: absolute, incredible joy.

Jesus is deeply concerned about those who are lost. In fact, He says they are the reason he left heaven to come to earth.[1] And in parables like those in Luke 15, He makes it clear that rescuing the lost is one of God's greatest concerns —and one of His deepest joys.

Rejoice! I have found my lost sheep.
Rejoice! I have found my lost coin.
Rejoice! My son was lost and now is found.

Jesus wants us to care about the lost, too. After He rose from the dead, His last instructions to His followers before ascending into heaven were, "Go into all the world and preach the gospel to every creature."[2] Preaching the gospel simply means sharing the good news—the best news—about Jesus Christ. And "all the world" begins where we are.

Where we live.

Where we work.

Where we play.

Have you ever stopped to think that Jesus didn't *have* to involve us in hHis project of saving the lost? One Sunday morning my pastor, Chad Garrison, pointed out that Jesus could have written John 3:16 in the stars in every language. He could send a personal e-mail to everyone on earth. But amazingly, Jesus asks us to tell others of His love instead.

What if someone invited you to attend the President's inaugural ball or to run with the Olympic torch or to say a prayer at a Billy Graham Crusade? Though you might feel a little intimidated at first and might need some instructions, wouldn't you be thrilled and honored to participate in such an event?

In comparison then, how do we respond when the King of kings invites us to participate in sharing the gospel with others? Shouldn't we feel just as thrilled and honored?

And sure, we might feel anxious or hesitant because we are uncertain what to do and because we don't want to offend anyone. These feelings are normal and even good, because they keep us sensitive to others and dependent on the Lord. But if we really want to follow God's heart, we need to find a way to move through the anxious feelings and reach out to those who need the good news we have to offer.

In the rest of this chapter, I'm going to share a few ideas that I've learned since that day when I saw "The Church Potluck" poster—approaches that have helped me find courage to talk about my relationship with Christ and trust the Lord for the results.

GENTLE PERSUASION

Jerry Larson, our very dear friend who was also our pastor for a dozen years, teaches wonderful evangelism seminars called His Touch: Lifestyle Evangelism through Gentle Persuasion.[3] After spending six hours with Jerry, not only are you equipped to share your faith, but you are *ready*—your engines are revved. The stories that come back to Jerry from seminar participants are absolutely astounding. And the *extraordinary* thing about the stories is that so many come to Christ when *ordinary* people start praying and sharing.

At the beginning of his seminars, Jerry makes it plain that prayer is the first and most essential commitment for anyone who wants to share Christ. We need to pray that God will become involved with people before we do, pray for the soil of hearts to be made ready, pray for blinders and barriers to be removed, and pray for effective communication. It's a good idea to request prayer from others, too, as the apostle Paul did in Ephesians 6:19: "Pray that I'll know what to say and have the courage to say it at the right time."[4]

After prayer, the second commitment is to spend more time with non-Christians. Connect with them where they feel comfortable, whether it's at Starbuck's, the golf course, a backyard barbeque, or a scrapbooking all-nighter. Be interested in the things they care about, learn about their jobs and hobbies and kids and where they grew up. Pick up their mail and feed their cat when they go on vacation. Take soup when they're sick. And love them. Love them to Christ.

> *I've seen Christians who've broken nearly every rule of communication and yet have been effective evangelists because they genuinely loved the person they were talking to. Ultimately, love is everything.*
>
> REBECCA MANLEY PIPPERT

It's wonderfully practical and profoundly effective. No room for strong-arm techniques, just gentle persuasion. With that approach, even the most timid people can become evangelists.

I'm always inspired when I remember a story I once heard on the radio. It was about a widower in his seventies, whom I'll call Mr. Samuels.

Every Tuesday morning, Mr. Samuels would stand at his front window waiting for the trash truck to come down the street. As soon as he saw it turn the corner, he went into action. When the truck pulled up on hot sultry days, he would be standing at the curb with lemonade. On cold, blustery days, he waited with hot chocolate. He'd find out what was new with the driver's family and talk for a few minutes about some current sports event. Week in and week out, the widower never missed a Tuesday.

One spring morning near Easter Sunday, Mr. Samuels invited the truck driver and his family to church. The man said he would really like to go, but he didn't have a suit to wear. Mr. Samuels told him that wouldn't matter. But when he realized how important a suit was to the driver, the widower bought him one and wrapped it up as a gift.

The truck driver came to church on Easter, along with his wife and all his children. And they kept coming week in and week out, as faithfully as Mr. Samuels had waited at the curbside. It wasn't long before the driver and all his family received Christ as their Savior. And all it took to make a connection was hot chocolate, lemonade, and a little gentle persuasion.

When They Ask

Sometimes when you start connecting with new friends, they might come right out and ask why you seem different or why you can have peaceful hope when your world (and the whole world for that matter) is falling apart. These are the most wonderful times of all—when your life is attractive enough for people to ask about it. First Peter 3:15 tells us that if we are asked about our Christian hope, we should always be ready to explain it.[5] But what does being ready really mean?

I think you should be prepared to tell *your personal story*—briefly. In three or four minutes, share the highlights of what was going on in your life before you came to know Christ and what changes you see in your life now. Tell when and how you came into a personal relationship with Christ. If you have been a committed Christian since childhood, share about how your parents raised you and how that has affected your life. Then talk about some of the heartbreaks and struggles you have experienced and how trusting Christ helped you through the darkest times.

Some people suggest practicing your story ahead of time so you can think through how to tell it without using words that non-Christians would have trouble understanding. Instead of speaking Christianese (the terms we learn at church but the rest of the world doesn't understand), you'll want to use more colloquial phrases.

I've discovered that even something as normal to Christians as referring to the Bible as God's Word could be confusing to a nonchurched person. One time a woman asked me which "specific word" God had given me. With her religious background, she thought that when I spoke of God's Word, I was referring to something like a mantra—a sacred word that she could recite over and over to gain access to certain cosmic forces.

New believers probably reach more non-Christians than anyone else. Part of the reason is that they are not so conditioned in Christianese as those who have been Christians a long time—they still speak the language of the nonbeliever. But more important, I think, is that new believers tend to be upbeat and enthusiastic. They usually can't cite chapter and verse of Scripture, but they can paraphrase the heart of the gospel in four words: Christ died for me. And they know that's good news!

Five Key Salvation Verses

- *Romans 3:23*: "All have sinned and fall short of the glory of God."
- *Romans 6:23*: "The wages of sin is death, but the gift of God is eternal life in Christ Jesus our Lord."
- *Romans 5:8*: "But God demonstrates His own love toward us, in that while we were still sinners, Christ died for us."
- *Romans 10:9–10*: "If you confess with your mouth the Lord Jesus and believe in your heart that God has raised Him from the dead, you will be saved. For with the heart one believes unto righteousness, and with the mouth confession is made unto salvation."
- *Romans 8:38–39*: "I am persuaded that neither death nor life, nor angels nor principalities nor powers, nor things present nor things to come, nor height nor depth, nor any other created thing, shall be able to separate us from the love of God which is in Christ Jesus our Lord."

Even though I admire the contagious spontaneity of new believers, the Gospel message as presented in the Bible gives the authority and power for everything we believe. For that reason, whether you are a new believer or a longtime Christian, it makes sense to prepare yourself to share the gospel message as it appears in God's Love Letter.

Both my husband and I have flagged all our Bibles with five key verses that help us when we are sharing God's plan of salvation. (They're listed on the previous page.) Inside the front cover of our Bibles, we've written a note to ourselves that says, "Start with Romans 3:23." Then in the page margin next to Romans 3:23 there is another note that says, "Go to Romans 6:23," and so forth through all five verses.

We started this practice when we were fairly new Christians. And although we eventually learned to quote these verses from memory or to paraphrase them accurately, we still flag our new Bibles in the same way. Our little prompters give us that extra bit of security in case we have a brain-freeze or senior moment. For us, they're an important part of being ready when someone asks about our Christian hope.

Let me end this section with some advice that Jerry Larson gave during the question-and-answer part of one of his evangelism seminars. A young man in his early twenties asked what to do when he really wanted to talk to his friend about his faith, but no matter how much he prepared, he still broke out in a sweat and got all tongue-tied just thinking about it.

"I would be real honest," Jerry suggested. "Just tell your friend that you would like to share the most important thing that has ever happened in your life, but that you get nervous whenever you try to do so. Then offer your friend a really good salvation pamphlet and tell him that after he has read it, you would like to talk more."[6]

Don't you love it? With just a little advance strategy, even the most tongue-tied, scared person can find a way to share the Good News.

OUR PART AND GOD'S PART

I didn't become a Christian until I was twenty-nine years old. About a month later, on a beautiful autumn morning, Carol stopped by our home unexpectedly. She wasn't a close friend, just part of a group of couples that occasionally got together to water ski or socialize. We had seen each other at a picnic the weekend before, but that had been the first time in months, and we'd barely talked then. So, when I opened the door, I was completely surprised to see Carol standing there.

"I was just driving down your street," she said, "and I wanted to stop in and ask you something. Is this an okay time?"

"Sure, come on in. The coffee's on."

My thoughts were bouncing around like crazy while I poured the coffee, because I couldn't imagine what she wanted to ask me. As soon as we sat down at the kitchen table, Carol wrapped her hands around her mug, leaned forward, and said, "I noticed something different about you at the picnic, and I'm just wondering what has changed."

Oh, my goodness. Panic. No one had told me that anything like this would happen, and I didn't have a clue of what to say. In fact, to this day I'm not sure what I *did* say. The best I can remember is that I told Carol about my sister and some people at our new church who had explained to me what it meant to have a personal relationship with Christ. I said that although I didn't understand everything, I knew for sure that Jesus is the only way to heaven, and that I had asked Him into my life and now was trying to live in a way that would please Him.

Then I took a deep breath and muttered a few words that sounded something like a couple of the Bible verses that my sister had shared with me. Even though Carol nodded her head a few times, I couldn't tell if I was making any sense. She kept her hands around her mug the whole time, and I don't think she drank a single drop of coffee.

I didn't ask Carol if she wanted Jesus to be part of her life, because I didn't know how to do that. I didn't even think to invite her to church or to give her a Bible. She hugged me when she left, and we talked about getting together, but Carol and her husband separated a few weeks later, and she moved away.

I still think about Carol and pray for her from time to time. In my heart I believe that in some miraculous way the Lord honored those tiny seeds of faith that I scattered on that unexpected autumn morning. Perhaps He brought someone else into Carol's life who watered the seeds, and then one day Jesus Himself brought forth a harvest. Maybe the next time Carol and I share mugs of coffee, it will be in heaven.

Why do I think that? Because I've seen it happen so many times since then. I've learned that God is able to make good use of our small acts of grace, our fumbling efforts to share His gospel. And that's important to know, because one of the biggest deterrents to sharing our faith is the fact that we don't always see results.

We can pray for months, sometimes years, and the people we care about the most don't seem to be any closer to the Lord than when we first started praying for them. We share our story about what Christ means to us and how believing in Him has changed our lives, but our friends or family members feel their lives are just fine without changing. We take homemade muffins to welcome new neighbors and ask them over for coffee, but they aren't interested when we invite them to church. When elderly Aunt Martha is rushed to the hospital with chest pains, we visit every day, but she doesn't want to hear about "being ready to meet the Lord."

These are the times when we must remember that God is working behind the scenes in ways we do not know or understand. Coming to Christ is often a long process, not a single event.[7] So God might be using your efforts to nudge someone closer to the cross, and you don't even realize it. Ultimately, the results belong to Christ, for He is the one who draws people to Himself.[8]

> *What could be more enjoyable than having someone in heaven walk up and say, "Thank you. You're the one who invited me here"?*
>
> LARRY MOYER

I love a song by singer-songwriter Ray Boltz called "Thank You."[9] It describes a scene in heaven where people wait in a long line to thank someone for helping them get to heaven. Each person names a small kindness, a small seed planted, a gentle word spoken—acts we might think of as small or everyday or ordinary, but they made a difference in his or her life. Can you imagine the incredible joy if even one person were to come up to *you* in heaven and say, "Remember that time when you told me about Christ and I brushed you off? Well, I never forgot what you said, and part of the reason I'm here is because of you. I just want to say thank you."

Only God knows how many people will find their way to heaven because of something you did that communicated the gospel to them. Maybe you were the one who helped my friend Carol after she moved away. Or maybe you were the nurse in the hospital who spoke to someone's Aunt Martha. Maybe you were the one who did a kindness to the homeless man, and he saw Jesus through you. Maybe you rescued one of the people drowning in the lake while I was attending the church potluck. Maybe you told your neighbors that if you could wish them anything, you would wish them Jesus.

You see, dear one, your life *is* making a difference—a difference that reaches beyond the stars to heaven. Look for me in that vast line of people waiting to see you. I'll want to meet you face-to-face and wrap my arms around you and say thank you —thank you for making a difference in our world.

The Man from Sydney

I first heard this story many years ago on a Christian radio station in Canada. A few weeks later, I heard it again on a nationally syndicated Christian radio program in the United States. It is one of those incredible stories in which truth is truly stranger (and more wonderful) than fiction, so I just had to retell it here.

Even though it was still raining, more than seven hundred people crowded into the soggy tent in Liverpool, England, for the first night of the weeklong meetings. As the preacher looked out at the people who had come to worship, he noticed a woman sitting about twelve rows from the platform. Her eyes were closed, her face radiant, as she sang the old gospel hymns. When the music ended, the preacher motioned to her and asked, "Sister, do you have a word for the Lord?"

Without hesitating, she stood to her feet. "Yes, I do," she called back, her voice alive with excitement.

"Eight years ago, as I walked down George Street in Sydney, Australia, an old man in ragged clothes stopped me. 'Excuse me, ma'am,' he said. 'If you were to die tonight, where would you spend eternity?'

"I couldn't get his question out of my thoughts. Finally, I

talked to the pastor of one of the churches near my home. With his encouragement, I started reading the Bible and discovered what it means to become a Christian. Finally, one day I prayed and asked Jesus to forgive my sins and to come into my life as Lord and Savior.

"From that moment on I have never doubted that when I die, I will spend eternity in heaven with Him."

The crowd overflowed again on the second night of the crusade. This time when the preacher searched the sea of new faces, his eyes were drawn to a young man with long brown hair pulled back into a neat ponytail. "Brother," he asked, "do you have a testimony for the Lord?" The young man jumped to his feet.

"When I was stationed in Sydney, Australia, during my military service a few years back, an old man in ragged clothes came up to me and asked if I died that night, did I know where I'd spend eternity.

"Well, when I got back to the barracks, I couldn't go to sleep. I kept thinking about the things my Christian parents had taught me, the stories I had learned in Sunday school, the Bible my grandmother had given me on my eighth birthday. Early the next morning, while the other guys were still sleeping, I knelt beside my bunk and asked Jesus Christ into my life.

"Every day since then, I find more reasons to be thankful for what Jesus has done for me. It all came together because of that old stranger on a street in Sydney."

On the third night, the preacher noticed a woman rocking a baby in her arms. For some reason he felt compelled to ask her, "Sister, do you have a word for the Lord?"

With a gentle voice, so quiet that the preacher asked if she could speak a little louder, she began her story. "Two years ago I visited Sydney, Australia . . ." And once again came a remarkable story about an old man in ragged clothes who asked a stranger a simple question.

Two months later, the traveling preacher went to Sydney, Australia, to find the old man. For days he walked the downtown streets of Sydney. Then, late one afternoon, an old man in ragged clothes walked up to him and said, "Excuse me, sir. May I ask you a question?"

The old man's name was Mr. Jenner. Inviting him to sit down on a bus-stop bench, the preacher began telling Mr. Jenner about the three testimonies he had heard in Liverpool. All the while he was listening, the old man kept brushing away tears that spilled down his weathered cheeks.

When the preacher was finished, Mr. Jenner sat there a long time. Finally, he was able to speak, his voice husky with emotion. "More than ten years ago, I promised God I would talk to at least one person every day about Jesus Christ. Although I never got discouraged, in all these years, this is the first time I've known that what I do makes a difference."

Mr. Jenner stood up, shook the preacher's hand, and said, "God bless you, sir. Thank you so much for coming."

The old man walked away. Just before turning the corner, he stopped to talk to a young man in a tan business suit. "Excuse me, sir. May I ask you a question?"

A Gentle Touch
For discussion or journaling

He who has the Son has life; he who does not have the Son of God does not have life. These things I have written to you who believe in the name of the Son of God, that you may know that you have eternal life.

1 John 5:12–13

1. Name at least one thing you would feel comfortable doing to start connecting with someone in your neighborhood or at work.

2. If you were sharing *your* story with a non-Christian, what three to five points would you include?

3. From the following list, circle the words or phrases that you think an unchurched person might have difficulty understanding. Then consider how you might rephrase the ones you circle.

lost	gospel	spiritual
born again	religious	saving faith
salvation	grace	saved
redeemed	believe	sin

A Prayer from the Heart

Dear Lord,

When I have an opportunity to share about my Christian hope, help me to do it in a way that is both clear and appealing. Help me to remember that You are the One who actually rescues the lost; I'm just responsible for sharing the good news that rescue is available. And, Lord, please give me a deeper concern for those who are still strangers to Your love—for to introduce another to You is the dearest way of all to make a difference in my world. ♡

From My Heart to Yours

As I finish the final pages of this book, I am wondering if perhaps there might be some dear reader who does not yet know Jesus Christ as her Savior. You might be like I was—attending church, praying, serving in various ways, but at the same time realizing that something is missing from your life. I was almost thirty before I began to understand the meaning of the five salvation verses found on page 162. Finally, one night as I knelt beside my bed, I prayed something like this:

> Dear Jesus,
>
> I believe that You are the Son of God and that You gave Your life for me on the cross as payment for my sins. I believe that You rose from the dead and are alive today in heaven. Please forgive me for my sins and come into my life as Savior and Lord.
>
> Thank You for the gift of eternal life. Help me to obey You and walk with You here on earth until the day when I walk with You in heaven. Amen.

My life changed the night I responded to God's magnificent act of grace. It is my hope that if you have never asked Jesus into your life, you might do so today. Once you do, you will discover the absolute joy of walking in His footsteps and following His heart.

Alice Gray

Notes

CHAPTER 1: PARADE OF LIGHTS

1. Matthew 5:14–16, New Living Translation.
2. John 8:12.
3. Isaiah 9:2; 2 Corinthians 4:6.
4. Matthew 6:33, italics added.
5. I recommend a wonderful audio Bible called *The Word Becomes Flesh: The Complete New Testament Read by Women* (Nashville: Nelson Bibles, 2005). Various women involved in the Christian marketplace read the Scriptures on CD, and all their proceeds are donated to Mercy Ministries, an international outreach organization that helps restore the lives of young women dealing with major life issues.
6. The Amplified Bible.
7. Galatians 5:22–23.
8. Charles R. Swindoll, *Improving Your Serve* (Waco, Tex.: Word, 1981), 135.
9. Alice Gray and Marilyn McAuley, *Mirror, Mirror: What Is My Heart Reflecting?* (Grand Rapids, Mich.: Zondervan, 1986), 93. Used by permission of Marilyn McAuley. All rights reserved.
10. Isaiah 53:4–5, New Century Version.
11. From Max Lucado, *A Gentle Thunder: Hearing God through the Storm* (Nashville: W Publishing Group, 1995), 83. Reprinted by permission of W Publishing Group, a division of Thomas Nelson, Inc., Nashville, Tennessee. All rights reserved.
12. New Living Translation.

CHAPTER 2: WHEN DAISIES DANCE

1. Proverbs 25:11.
2. Philippians 2:4.
3. Romans 12:15, New American Standard Bible.
4. Story attributed to "author unknown" in Phyllis Hobe, ed., *Fragile Moments: When God Speaks in Whispers* (Old Tappan, N.J.: Revell, 1980), 1.
5. Ruth Graham with Stacey Mattingly, *In Every Pew Sits a Broken Heart: Hope for the Hurting* (Grand Rapids, Mich.: Zondervan, 2004).

6. Isaiah 40:11, 29 and Matthew 11:28–30.
7. 2 Corinthians 1:4.
8. Allison Harms, "Beauty Contest," in Alice Gray, comp., *Stories for the Family's Heart* (Sisters, Oreg.: Multnomah, 1998), 68. Used by permission of Allison Harms.
9. The Message.

CHAPTER 3: DAY BRIGHTENERS
1. Acts 20:35, The Message.
2. Steve Stephens and Alice Gray, *The Worn Out Woman: When Life Is Full and Your Spirit Is Empty* (Sisters, Oreg.: Multnomah, 2004), 101.
3. Matthew 8:3.
4. Ross Campbell, *How to Really Love Your Teenager*, rev. ed. (Wheaton, Ill.: Victor Books, 1993).
5. Galatians 6:2.
6. Adapted from Stephens and Gray, *Worn Out Woman*, 104–5.
7. Candy Abbott, "Ivy's Cookies," reprinted from Jack Canfield, Mark Victor Hansen, and Tom Lagana, *Chicken Soup for the Prisoner's Soul: 101 Stories to Open the Heart and Rekindle the Spirit of Hope, Healing and Forgiveness* (Deerfield Beach, Fla.: Health Communications, 2000), 102–7. Also printed in Alice Gray, comp., *Stories for a Woman's Heart: Second Collection* (Sisters, Oreg.: Multnomah, 2001), 29–32. Used by permission of Candy Abbott.

CHAPTER 4: ONCE UPON A FRONT PORCH SWING
1. Excerpted from Kimber Annie Engstrom, "Front Porch Swing." Used by permission of the author. She can be contacted at kimmieq@bendbroadband.com.
2. Adapted from Alice Gray, Steve Stephens, and John Van Diest, comps., *Lists to Live By: The First Collection* (Sisters, Oreg.: Multnomah, 1999), 62–63. Used by permission of the author, Barbara Baumgardner.
3. Cheri Fuller, *Fragrance of Kindness* (Nashville: J. Countryman, 2000), 72.
4. Luke 10:27.
5. See Romans 12:13; Hebrews 13:2; 1 Peter 4:9–10; 3 John 1:5–8.
6. *Life Application Study Bible*, New Living Translation (Wheaton, Ill.: Tyndale House, 2004), 2110.
7. Romans 12:13.
8. Jane Jarrell, *Simple Hospitality* (Nashville: W Publishing Group, 2005); Ann Platz and Susan Wales, *The Pleasure of Your Company: Simple Ideas for Enjoyable Entertaining* (Eugene, Oreg.: Harvest

House, 1999); Emilie Barnes with Anne Christian Buchanan, *Welcome Home: Creating Your Own Place of Beauty and Love* (Eugene, Oreg.: Harvest House, 1997). *Welcome Home* has also been condensed into a gift book called *Home Warming: Secrets to Making Your House a Welcoming Place* (Eugene, Oreg.: Harvest House, 2005).

9. Condensed and adapted from Alice Gray and Susan Wales, *A Keepsake Christmas* (Nashville: J Countryman, 2005), 29. Used by permission of the authors.

10. Emilie Barnes, *The Spirit of Loveliness* (Eugene, Oreg.: Harvest House, 1992), 125–7. Copyright © 1999 by Harvest House Publishers, Eugene, Oreg.. Used by permission.

11. New International Version.

CHAPTER 5: HEARTS ENTWINED

1. Pamela Reeve, *Relationships: What It Takes to Be a Friend* (Sisters, Oreg.: Multnomah, 1997), 22–27.

2. Gale Berkowitz, "UCLA Study on Friendship among Women," © 2002, accessed on *Caduceus Online*, http://www.caduceus.info/News/newshealth.htm.

3. Condensed from chapter 11 of Steve Stephens and Alice Gray, *The Worn Out Woman: When Life Is Full and Your Spirit Is Empty*, Sisters, Oreg.: Multnomah, 2004), 130–5.

4. To read more about these biblical friendships, see the following passages. *Naomi and Ruth*: the entire book of Ruth. *David and Jonathan*: 1 Samuel 18–20. *Jesus and Mary, Martha, and Lazarus*: Luke 10:38–42 and John 11. Jesus and His disciples: all the Gospels, but especially Matthew 4:17–22; 8:14–15; 16:13–23; 17:1–8; 26:31–75; Mark 10:35–45; Luke 5:1–11; 9:28–33; 22:31–62; John 13:6–9; 31–37; 18:15–27; 19:25–27; 20:3–4; 21:1–24. *Paul and Timothy*: Acts 16:1–3; 1 Corinthians 4:16–17; 16:10; and the entire book of Timothy.

5. Ecclesiastes 4:9–10, 12, New Living Translation.

6. Mark 12:30–31, New American Standard Bible.

7. From Patsy Clairmont, Barbara Johnson, et al., *Irrepressible Hope* (Nashville: W Publishing Group, 2003), 160–61. Reprinted by permission of W Publishing, a division of Thomas Nelson, Inc., Nashville, Tennessee. All rights reserved.

CHAPTER 6: HEARTPRINTS AT HOME

1. Adapted from a story captured on the Internet. Author unknown.

2. Alice Gray, Steve Stephens, and John Van Diest, comps., *Lists to Live By for Every Caring Family* (Sisters, Oreg.: Multnomah, 2001), 43.

3. Deuteronomy 11:19.
4. Brenda Nixon, "Make Your Children Thirsty . . . for God," *Christian Women Today*, 2005, http://www.christianwomentoday.com/parenting/thirsty.html.
5. In Patsy Clairmont, Barbara Johnson, et al., *Irrepressible Hope*, (Nashville: W publishing Group, 2003), 14.
6. Condensed and retold from an anonymous story in Alice Gray, comp., *Stories for a Teen's Heart: Over One Hundred Treasures to Touch Your Soul* (Sisters, Oreg.: Multnomah, 1999), 267.
7. Dannah Gresh is a nationally recognized expert on teen sexuality and the founder of Pure Freedom. Quote is from Jane Johnson Struck, "Planned Purity," *Christian Parenting Today* 17, no. 4 (Summer 2005): 32.
8. James and Shirley Dobson, *Night Light for Parents* (Sisters, Oreg.: Multnomah, 2002), 167.
9. New Living Translation. Italics and hyphens are my additions.
10. Gary Smalley and John Trent, *Leaving the Light On* (Sisters, Oreg.: Multnomah, 1994).
11. Patty Duncan, "The Mailbox," *Christian Women Today*, 2005, http://www.christianwomentoday.com/womenmen/mailbox.html. Originally published in *The Lookout*, May 11, 1997.
12. New International Version.

CHAPTER 7: THE BEAUTY OF TIME
1. New Living Translation.
2. See Isaiah 25:4; Romans 8:38–39; and Psalm 23:4.
3. Ecclesiastes 3:1, 4.
4. Bruce Bickel, Cheryl Bickel, Stan Jantz, and Karin Jantz, *Life's Little Handbook of Wisdom* (Urichsville, Ohio: Barbour, 1992). Quoted in Alice Gray, Steve Stephens, and John Van Diest, comps., *Lists to Live By for Smart Living* (Sisters, Oreg.: Multnomah, 2002), 127.
5. March/April 2005. The women depicted are Joanne Woodward, age seventy-five; Shirley Jones, seventy; Kathy Bates, fifty-seven; Marcia Gay Harden, forty-five; Patty Duke, fifty-eight; Cloris Leachman, seventy-nine; and Rita Moreno, seventy-three.
6. Linda Anderson, *Slices of Life* (Grand Rapids, Mich.: Baker Book House, 1986), 238–40. Used by permission of the author.

CHAPTER 8: EVEN THE LEAST
1. New Living Translation.
2. Camerin Courtney, "Steps of Faith," *Today's Christian Woman*,

July/August 2005, 44. For more information on the Averill's ministry, visit www.footprintsministry.com.
3. Susan Fahncke, "The Tattooed Stranger," quoted in Alice Gray, comp., *Stories for a Faithful Heart* (Sisters, Oreg.: Multnomah, 2000), 30–32. Used by permission of the author. For more about Susan Fahncke, see her Web site: www.2theheart.com.
4. New Living Translation.

CHAPTER 9: LOST AND FOUND
1. Matthew 18:11–14; Luke 19:10.
2. Mark 16:15.
3. For information about His Touch seminars, contact Jerry Larson at 509-465-3206.
4. The Message.
5. New Living Translation.
6. I recommend one from the Billy Graham Evangelistic Association called *Steps to Peace with God* (Minneapolis: World Wide Publications, 1998).
7. 1 Corinthians 3:5–7.
8. John 6:44.
9. You can hear this great song on the CD, *Thank You* (Sony, 1994) or the compilation *Moments for the Heart: The Very Best of Ray Boltz* (Ray Boltz Music, 2002). Look for his CDs at your local Christian bookstore or online at www.rayboltz.com.

ABOUT THE AUTHOR

Alice Gray is best known for her seven-million copy, best-selling series, Stories for the Heart that has won her many awards and honors. An inspirational conference speaker and radio and television guest, Alice has been inspiring women for more than two decades. She is a mother, a grandmother, and lives with her husband, Al, in Arizona.

Also available from Alice Gray

ISBN: 0849904374

$10.99

*A*s much as we long for blue skies and smooth sailing, storms and rocky times are inevitably a part of our lives. Sometimes the storms hit suddenly and fiercely, leaving behind terrible devastation. Other times the storms are silent clouds of desperation lingering on the horizon, threatening to rock everything we hold dear. Often, hope is the only comfort and joy we can know in the midst of these hard times.

W PUBLISHING GROUP
A Division of Thomas Nelson Publishers
Since 1798
www.wpublishinggroup.com